THE USBORNE OFFICIAL

SPY'S HANDBOOK

Illustrated by Colin King

Contributors:
Falcon Travis, Judy Hindley,
Ruth Thomson, Heather Amery,
Christopher Rawson and Anita Harper

About this book

This is a book for anyone who wants to be a Good Spy. It shows every skill a Good Spy needs, including how to write code messages, how to put on disguises, and how to stalk and shadow Enemy Spies secretly.

Good Spies must always be on guard for Enemy Spies. They need hiding places for their messages, and tricks to 'cover' or disguise their meetings. They must know how to change their looks with special clothes and make-up, and how to act a part successfully while in disguise.

And all the time, they must be looking out for the chance to fool Enemy Spies and learn their secrets. Keep this book handy at all times, so that you can check your codes and signals whenever necessary — and keep your secrets out of the hands of the Enemy.

Usborne Quicklinks

For links to websites where you can find more detective activities, go to www.usborne.com/quicklinks and type the keywords "spy's handbook".

Please read our internet safety guidelines on the Usborne Quicklinks website.

Contents

Passing secret messages

A Good Spy and his Contact know how to exchange messages secretly. They may need to pass on information about Enemy plans (this sort of message is usually written in secret code). Or they may need to arrange secret meetings or pass on warnings of dangers or emergencies.

Spy messages should never be exchanged openly. It is dangerous to meet your Contact often, or to be seen exchanging papers. Remember: you never know when the Enemy may be watching...

This picture gallery is really a place where spies rendezvous (meet by arrangement).

They pretend they have come to see the pictures — hoping to put the Enemy off the scent.

If they think they are being watched, they put emergency plans into operation . . . .

. . . and secretly exchange their messages without even showing that they know each other.

Good Spies exchange messages so secretly that Enemy Spies never see them do it — and may not even suspect that they know each other. Below you can see some of the ways they work together.

If you set up a spy ring (a group of spies who work together) it is a good idea to work out several plans like this, as well as emergency signals for a quick change of plan. Later in the book you'll find hints on how to do this.

This spy never meets his Contact, but he often goes to the library that his Contact uses.

The librarian is really a letter box (someone who keeps messages for spies). She passes on the message.

This spy never meets his Contact. He leaves him messages at a spot they have agreed on.

In spy language this is called a 'drop'. Later his Contact visits the drop and collects the message.

Using drops

You must have several drops in case one is found by an Enemy. You also need another spot, or signpost, to leave your Contact a signal saying which drop you've used. Each should be out of sight of the others, so the Enemy can't watch them all at once.

1. DROP 1.
(HIDDEN BY A BEND IN THE PATH).

FOLLOW THE SPY TO SEE HOW HE PLANS HIS ROUTE

4. SIGNPOST (KNOTTED-STRING-SIGNAL ON TWIG)

Choosing a drop

Find a spot where you can be hidden from view for a short time, without looking suspicious. Look carefully, watching how people come and go, and what happens at different times of the day. Approach your drop from all directions, to work out when and how a passerby might catch a glimpse of you. Will you see them coming? What can you do to avoid them? Then find a good hiding place there. See pages 22 and 23 for more ideas.

When leaving a message, plan your route so that if one drop looks risky you can go to the others. Walk slowly, stopping to look at the flowers or birds, in case you are being followed. Go to the signpost last, and leave a signal to show where the message is.

2. DROP 2.
(HOLLOW LOG)

3. DROP 3.

Using a signpost

Decide with your Contact on a few simple signals to leave at the signpost to tell him which drop you have used — perhaps a chalk mark or a coded matchstick. Pages 14-15 show lots of signals which the Enemy may never even notice. Your Contact must always remove the signal at the signpost before he collects the message at the drop. To find out if he has got the message, walk past the signpost and check if your signal has now gone.

Danger park

Each of the spies shown here is about to leave a message at his drop (shown as a star). Some have chosen badly — and may be in danger. Would you have made the same mistakes? Try to spot the dangerous drops yourself — then turn the page to check the things you have noticed.

Danger park solution

These are the dangerous drops:

A The spy is well-covered here—but so is anyone following him. There are so many turnings that it would be impossible for him to make sure that no one is near.

B The stretch of path in both directions means the spy can be seen from far away. If anyone is coming, he will have to wait a suspiciously long time before he is alone.

C To dodge away from the main path into one that leads nowhere will arouse suspicion ...

D ... particularly if you do it again and again.

E This spy can never know if he is being watched from the building opposite. Someone from the Enemy camp may be standing back from the window of an unlit room on the upper floor, following his every move.

These are the good drops:

1 The spy can quickly check all the nearby paths, and the curved shrubbery covers him, even from a short distance away. If he has to wait for a while, he can pretend to be looking at the statue.

2 This spy also has good cover and he can easily check all approaches before he acts. The pond is a good excuse to hang around.

3 If the spy comes in from the main path (the one leading to the statue) and walks halfway around, he can check the whole area.

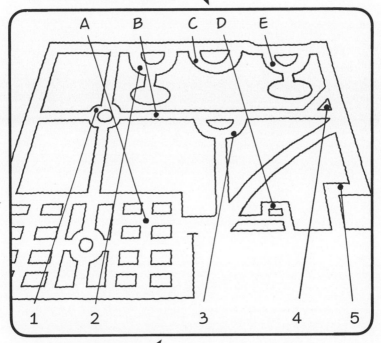

DANGEROUS DROPS

A   B   C   D   E

1   2   3   4   5

GOOD DROPS

4 Anywhere along the inside of this wall would make a good drop. From either end, the spy can see a long distance away — and he can hide quickly. But he should go from one end of the wall to the other, checking all approaches, before he takes action.

5 There is a good lookout point at each end of this stretch of path, too. From these points the spy can see anyone coming from a long way away. If the spy sees a passerby in the distance, he may have time to hide the message before he arrives.

Signpost leaf code

Your signpost need not be as secret as a drop. A Good Spy knows how to leave signals that hardly anyone will notice, and only his Contact will understand. The leaf code below is a good example.

Just be sure to put the leaf in a spot where your Contact can see it but where it will not blow away. You and your Contact should each write down the signals and what they mean, as shown here. (This is your code book.)

CODE BOOK

SFB-MESSAGE AT DROP 1

TEAR OFF A BIT OF LEAF TO LENGTHEN THE STALK

BACK VIEW

SFB (STALK THROUGH LEAF, FROM THE FRONT TO THE BACK) — MESSAGE AT DROP 1.

SBF (STALK THROUGH LEAF, BACK TO FRONT) — MESSAGE AT DROP 2.

TBS (TWIG-ENDS AT BACK, SIDEWAYS) — MESSAGE AT DROP 3.

TFS (TWIG-ENDS AT FRONT, SIDEWAYS) — NO MESSAGE.

SPY TRICK

PRETEND TO BE IDLY FIDDLING WITH A LEAF...

... SECRETLY MARK IT AND LEAVE IT IN A SPECIAL SPOT.

YOUR CONTACT PICKS IT UP TO FIND WHICH DROP YOU'VE USED.

LATER YOU CAN CHECK TO SEE IF IT'S GONE ...

... OR REPLACED BY A NEW SIGNAL.

COLLECT ANY SIGNAL LEFT BY YOUR CONTACT.

TSF (TWIG THROUGH STALK-LOOP AT FRONT) — MESSAGE NOT FOUND.

TSB (TWIG THROUGH STALK-LOOP AT BACK) — AVOID DROPS — MEET AT HIDEOUT.

TBL (TWIG ENDS AT BACK, LENGTHWAYS) — AVOID DROPS — RETURN TOMORROW.

TFL (TWIG-ENDS AT FRONT, LENGTHWAYS) — LEAVE QUICKLY — WE ARE DISCOVERED.

Signpost tactics

These spies are using several kinds of signpost signals. (The next pages show a code for each.) If you make chalk marks, use a dull shade that won't attract attention. Put coded stones or matchsticks where they won't be disturbed. Then remove your Contact's signals quickly and secretly, as shown.

RUB OUT CHALK MARK ON LEDGE

SHOE OF SPY USING GROUND LEVEL TACTICS

THE ENDS OF THE MATCHES ARE A SIGNAL. PUSH THEM INTO THE GROUND

KNOTS IN THE STRING ARE A SIGN (COLLECT

THE MARKS ON THE MATCHSTICK ARE A SIGNAL (COLLECT)

Ground level tactics

If you have to bend over or kneel down to put a signal in place, or to pick one up, always try to think of a reason for doing it. For example, pretend a shoelace has come undone and you need to tie it, or you need to pull up your socks. Or limp a bit as you get near the signpost, then stop and pretend to remove a pebble from your shoe. If you are carrying something, you could pretend it is so heavy that you have to put it down and rest a bit.

Always behave casually while waiting for the right moment to use your signpost. With practice you will be able to use it even when you are under observation (being watched). Learn to memorize things like chalk signals at a glance. You can check their meaning in your code book later.

PRETEND TO TRAIL YOUR HAND ON RAILINGS WHILE YOU SLIP OFF CODE STRING

THIS CHALK MARK IS A SIGNAL— RUB IT OUT

MARKS ON STONE ARE A SIGNAL. (COLLECT)

Special signpost code

The meaning of each of these signpost codes is shown by just two signals—dots and dashes, long and short knots, or heads and tails of matchsticks.

Choose whichever is easiest to use at your signpost. Both you and your Contact should write out the meanings and keep them in a secret notebook like this.

Here are four different ways of making the dot-and-dash messages.

Use a black dot to show the head of a match and a circle for the tail. Write L for a long knot and S for a short knot.

1 MESSAGE AT DROP Q

2 MESSAGE AT DROP X

3 MESSAGE AT DROP Z

4 AVOID DROPS PLAN NO.1

5 AVOID DROPS PLAN NO.2

6 MESSAGE NOT FOUND

The dot-and-dash code can be used in lots of ways—chalked on a wall or a small stone, or even written on a matchstick laid on its side.

Push the head-and-tail matchsticks into the earth in some protected spot—next to a wall, for instance. You could hang a knotted string message over a twig or some railings.

Loop the string like this.
Then pull it tight.

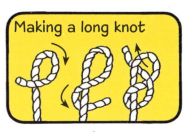

Loop the string like this.
Then pull it tight.

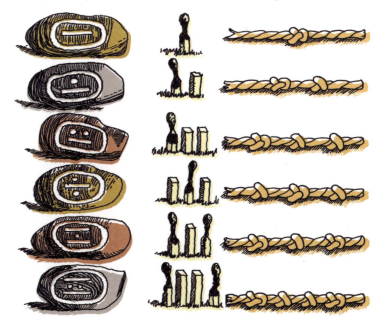

Quick message codes

Use these codes to keep your messages secret.
Each scrambles the letters in a special way.
The code initials give your Contact a key.

Rev-Random
Write the message backwards (1).
Then break it into new groups (2).

SPIES ON RADIO

1. OIDAR NO SEIPS
2. OI DAR NO SEIPS

Bi-Rev
Pair up the letters (1). Then write
each pair backwards (2).

1. (SP(IE)(S O)(N R)(AD) (IO)

2. (PS)(EI)(O S)(R N)(DA)(OI)

Rev-Groups
Group the message letters differently
(1). Write each group backwards (2).

1. SPI ESON RA DIO
2. IPS NOSE AR OID

Mid-Null
Break the message into
even-numbered groups of letters (1).
Split each group into halves (2).
Put a dummy letter (a null) between
the halves in each group (3).

1. SP IE SONRAD IO

2. S P I E SON RAD 1 O

3. SUP ICE SONDRAD IDO

Sandwich
Write out the first half of the
message, leaving spaces between
letters (1). Write the second half in
the spaces (2). Then group the letters
differently (3).

1. S   P   I   E   S   O

2. S N P R I A E D S I O O

3. SNPRI AE DSIOO

Pendulum
Regroup the message letters (1). Mark
a space for each. Write the first of
each group in the middle space (2).
Add the rest from left to right as
shown (3).

1. SPIES ONRA DIO
2. _S_   _O_ _D_
3. PS   ____ ____
    PSI
    EPSI

If you receive a message and your Contact forgets to give you the key to the code, try these ways of finding which code he or she used.

OI DAR NO SEIPS

Start writing the message letters from the end and see if they begin to form into words.

PSEIO SR NDAOI

Try reversing the first few pairs of letters in each group and look for words.

IPS NOSE AR OID

Try reversing the letters in each group and look for words.

SUP ICE SONDRAD IDO

Cross out the middle letter in the first few groups. Try joining the rest of the letters into words.

SNPRI AE DSIOO

Starting with the first letter, write every other letter. Then add the letters in between.

EPSIS ANOR IDO

Write the middle letter of the first group. Add the first letter to the left, then the first to the right, then the second to the left, and so on. Can you see a word?

Who is the traitor?

The four spies shown below are members of an international spy ring. One of them has betrayed their leader, who has been captured. Who is the traitor and who will be the new leader?

Decode their messages (written in Quick Codes) to work out who they are. Check your answers on page 190.

PARIS CALLING DELHI

ELRUO ACSIREDA GU
WOTH ESSIL MOCHIDNOC
ADNAM OYER WOU L.

DELHI CALLING PARIS

EOYMCD SEANMI
LOONTW RTATHTERIO
OSIFX XFIHWOSO

DELHI CALLING CAIRO

OFI XA S RTIAOTB
RTA NKWOH SMI A
IN MTO ABW TOH SI

CAIRO CALLING DELHI

CUOT DMEIN NAEMIE
SS NSEHIO TUH
LEDR BB EASTENC
ORR EFT OBX

HOT TIP

You have discovered that the code names of the four spies are Owl, Elk, Bat and Fox. (Look for these letters to help you decode the messages more quickly.)

None of the spies (except the leader) is supposed to know which code names belong to the other spies. But both the traitor and the new leader have dropped enough clues for you to work out who they are.

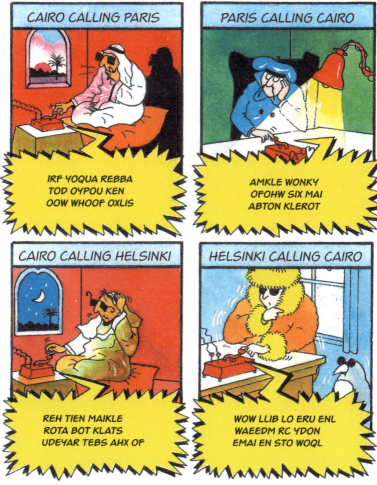

CAIRO CALLING PARIS

IRF YOQUA REBBA
TOD OYPOU KEN
OOW WHOOF OXLIS

PARIS CALLING CAIRO

AMKLE WONKY
OFOHW SIX MAI
ABTON KLEROT

CAIRO CALLING HELSINKI

REH TIEN MAIKLE
ROTA BOT KLATS
UDEYAR TEBS AHX OF

HELSINKI CALLING CAIRO

WOW LLIB LO ERU ENL
WAEEDM RC YDON
EMAI EN STO WOQL

Hiding a message

Good Spies are always on the lookout for new places to hide their secret messages. Here are some ideas for places to hide them and ways to disguise them as leaves or twigs. Each arrow in the picture points to a hiding place.

If a bit of a message sticks out, rub it with earth to camouflage it. Decide with your Contact exactly where your hiding place will be—make sure you choose one you will both be able to find again.

Hiding places

1. Under the root of a tree or a bush.

2. In the cleft of a tree or a bush, or slipped into a crack in a wooden fence or gatepost.

3. Under a hedge or bush, disguised as a leaf or a twig, or rolled up in some clay.

4. Stuck under a bench.

5. Behind a plaque.

1 Preparing the message

ROLL UP

TIE THREAD AND TRIM

Roll up the message tightly to make it less noticeable and easier for your Contact to get hold of. Tie it up with thread or a rubber band.

RUB ON DIRT TO CAMOUFLAGE

If you put the message in a very narrow place, leave a small part of the thread sticking out. Your Contact can use this to pull it out.

Leaf disguise

ROLL UP

STORE IN BOX

Roll a leaf around a pencil and tie it with thread until it is dry. Keep it in a matchbox until you need to use it.

Twig disguise

TWIST

TWIST SANDPAPER

6. Under creeping plants or lifted turf or moss.

7. Between the stones of the pedestal of a statue.

8. Under a loose paving stone.

Bore a hole through the soft middle of a short bit of garden cane. Then twist rolled-up sandpaper inside to finish hollowing it out.

Pocket code card

This code card folds up small enough to fit into a matchbox, but you can make 12 different codes with it. In each code, every letter or number of the message is swapped with another letter, or a different number. The pattern is below.

Special ways of folding the card show different alphabets. These are marked with key numbers on the edge. Be sure to tell your Contact which key number you used.

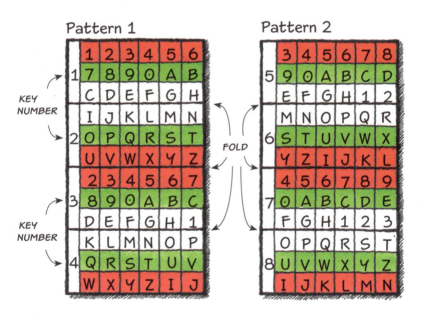

Use thin cardboard or stiff paper, just the size shown here. Draw the lines and shade them. Copy the letters and numbers exactly like Pattern 1 on one side. Turn the card over and upside-down. Now copy Pattern 2 on it. Use three different shades. Any will do but be sure to change the shade from row to row, as in the patterns.

Folds to use

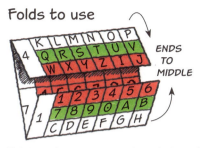

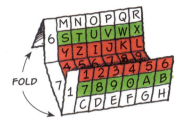

Fold in half to see codes 1-2, 3-4. Fold the other way for 5-6, 7-8. The ends-to-middle fold shows codes 4-1, 2-3, 6-7 and 8-5.

Fold the top edge down and the bottom edge up for codes 2-5 and 6-1. Fold the other way around for codes 4-7 and 8-3.

How it works

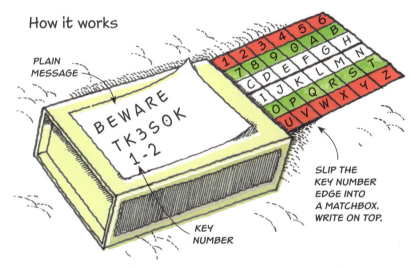

PLAIN MESSAGE

BEWARE
TK3SOK
1-2

KEY NUMBER

SLIP THE KEY NUMBER EDGE INTO A MATCHBOX. WRITE ON TOP.

To encode a message, first print it out plain, as shown here. (A message not in code is called 'plain' or 'clear'.) Choose your key number. Under each letter of the message, print the letter or number in the same column in the same shade, moving up or down. For example, in the 1-2 code shown here, the code letter for B is T and the code letter for E is K.

To decode a message, you do the same thing. Fold the card to show the key numbers. Then, under each code letter, or number, print the letter in the same shade in the same column.

Code breaking practice

Good Spies test their skill and keep in practice by exchanging coded messages. Experienced code breakers use complicated codes and make their messages as difficult to break as possible. New code breakers start with easier codes and may even give each other hints and clues.

To begin with, try some simple substitution codes. These are codes in which the message letters are swapped with the letters of a specially scrambled alphabet—like those on the code card on page 24, or the keyword alphabets on page 58. To help your partner you can put in a clue, like the name of a month, a day of the week, or a compass point.

Try decoding the message below to see how it works. It is written in an alphabet on the code card. Clue: the second word is a number from one to ten.

> 2RO 2RHOO 80A 7O7XOH1 EP E9H 1FC H38Q A366
>
> 7OO2 91 W2 ROWZG9WH2OH1 2E83QR2

Tips for code breakers

When decoding a message, write it in large block letters with lots of space below each line. When you find the plain letter meaning of a code letter, write it under the code letter all through the message.

Try to find vowels (AEIOU and Y), because every word has at least one. Look for one-letter words, which must be A or I or (very occasionally) O.

Double letters might be OO or EE (the most common double vowels). Another common pair of letters is TH. The most common 3-letter group (as a word or part of a word) is THE.

Punctuation marks help the code breaker, so don't use them in coded messages. For example, OR, AND and BUT often come after commas, while THAT, WHO and WHICH often come before. A sentence ending in a question mark begins with W.

Look with a code breaker's eye. Note patterns of double and repeated letters—as in tomORROw, LEvEL, lETTEr and CHurCH.

Code breaking contests

This game is for three or more people. One person (the challenger) secretly encodes a message, while the others try to break the code.

The challenger uses a code made with a secret keyword (see page 58). He or she writes the plain message with the code letters below. Then the challenger calls out the code letters of each word for the others to write down. Each message should be at least 15 words long, with the code letters in the same groups as the plain words.

Each code breaker starts with ten points. He or she can secretly ask the challenger the meaning of any word, but loses a point each time. The person who works out the whole message while losing the fewest points is the winner.

Check your security

A successful Spy Ring must check that their security is good. There are some ways to find out if you are being watched when you are in your drop area to deliver or collect a message.

If you know you are being followed, then you must find out if the person following you is really a member of an Enemy spy ring. The trick is to make Enemy Spies give themselves away and keep them guessing about your drops.

Never look directly at a suspect unless you are sure he is not looking at you, or cannot see you.

Pretend you are not interested in him, or have not even noticed that he is there at all.

A suspect may watch you only because he has seen you watching him. If so, get out of sight and show no more interest in him.

If the suspect is watching you, make it obvious that you are watching him. He will probably disappear and be more careful.

1 Checking a suspect

Choose a false drop away from the real drops, which you can watch. Hide nothing here.

2

Get the suspect to follow you. Look as suspicious as you can, without giving yourself away.

3

When you are sure you are being followed, lead the suspect to the false drop in a roundabout way.

4

Go to the drop but do not let the suspect see if you are delivering or collecting a message.

5

When you have left, the suspect will check the drop. As it is empty, he will think you were collecting a message.

6

The suspect has now given himself away. He will watch the false drop for a delivery and you can just disappear from the scene.

Checking for interception

If Enemy agents have discovered your real drops, they will read the messages and put them back. Then they will copy the messages and try to break the codes. This is called interception. Because the messages have been replaced, you won't know they've been read unless you check. Here are some ways to check if messages have been intercepted.

1 Paper or thread test

Fold up the message. Open it out again and put two tiny bits of white paper or thread in the first crease. Fold it and put more paper or thread in the second crease.

2

Finish folding the message. Check later by opening the paper to see if the bits are still there. If they aren't, they must have fallen out when opened by an interceptor.

Glue test

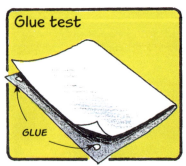

GLUE

Seal the corners of the first fold with tiny dots of glue. Then fold up the message. The seals break easily when the paper is opened. Check messages for broken seals.

Jam test

WIPE JAM UNTIL THIN ENOUGH NOT TO SHOW

Fold up a message and open it out. Smear jam thinly on half of the back of the paper. Any fingerprints will show up on the jam. Do not touch it with your own fingers.

Broken codes

You know that messages are being read by the Enemy. But have they broken your codes? Here is a way to find out.

Spoof code

Write a message in a code you suspect has been broken, saying future messages will be at a new drop. Say where the drop is, and what code will be used. Write a message in this new 'Spoof' Code.

Spoof drop

Hide the paper at the new 'Spoof' Drop. Use one of the message checks. You musn't be seen or you won't know if it was the message in the broken code that sent the Enemy there.

Fooling the enemy

If you know that your codes are being broken and your drops intercepted, this is how to fool the Enemy Spies. Find a new drop. Use different codes. New drops should be out of sight of the intercepted one. To keep the Enemy agents from suspecting you have changed drops, leave messages in a Spoof Code at the old drops. Get different Couriers to deliver and collect messages as usual, leaving plenty of time for them to be intercepted.

Vanishing secrets

Here is a good way to keep secret routes marked on a sketch map. You can also use it for a map of your secret drops, places to meet Contacts, or even spots where Enemy agents are thought to be operating. The marks are invisible, but you can make them appear whenever you need to check the map.

You can also use these vanishing marks for keeping secret notes, such as the code names of Contacts or their telephone numbers.

Draw a map in pencil of the area to cover. Put in landmarks, such as a school or park.

Wet the map all over with cold water. Lay it down flat on a newspaper. Put clean paper on top.

Draw in the route or drops with a pencil, pressing hard. When the map dries the marks will vanish.

Wet the map again and the secret routes or marks will appear. Dry the map to make them disappear.

Spy test

You have been captured and imprisoned by the Enemy. The situation seems nearly hopeless. You have no weapons nor spy equipment—only what is shown in the picture below. Your captors have allowed you to write one letter, but you know it must not look at all suspicious. Not even the cleverest code will fool them. How can you use this letter to send a message to your Spy Ring asking for help? Turn the page and see . . .

Invisible inks

Your captors don't know that 'Mother' is the codename of your spy chief, and that you have all you need to write an invisible message between the lines of your letter. In fact, you have three methods to choose. Read on and see. . . .

Matchstick pen

Sharpen the end of a matchstick by rubbing it on a rough stone. (Sandpaper works even better.)

Spit method

WRITE BETWEEN THE LINES OF A LETTER, OR ON THE BACK LIKE THIS

Wet the matchstick with spit and write lightly, as shown. Hold the paper to the light to check what you have written.

Juice method

Poke the fleshy bit of the apple core with the matchstick to collect some juice. Write with the juice.

1 Wax method

WAX DRIPS

CHIP OFF

Carefully chip away some of the candle drips. Try to break off some long, thin pieces.

2

HOLD IN ONE HAND

ROLL WITH OTHER HAND

Use the heat of your hands to warm the wax. Roll the bits into a pencil shape. Write with it.

1 Letter signals

The initials used in the address of the letter are a signal to Mother that the letter contains an urgent secret message.

2

Clues in the letter tell Mother how to develop it. The next pages show how to plant these clues (called indicators).

Spit developing

To see the spit message, the spy chief must brush the paper with watery ink. The message shows up as a slightly darker shade.

Wax developing *GIVE A GENTLE SHAKE*

To see the wax message, he sprinkles the paper with chalk dust, then shakes it off. The chalk sticks only to the wax.

Juice developing *COOKED JUICE BECOMES LIGHT BROWN*

To see the juice message, he heats it in a cool oven (about 120° C, 250° F, Gas Mark 2) so that the juice warms up and darkens.

Action!

The message tells him where you are and the plan of the building where you are imprisoned, so he can organize your escape.

Secret indicators

Letters to other members of your Good Spy Ring
should contain special clues to show them what to
expect. Here is a good system to use—make sure
everyone knows what the clues mean.

INVISIBLE MESSAGE
INDICATOR

Thursday 1pm

PHONEY
INITIAL. THE SPY'S
REAL MIDDLE NAME IS
EDWARD

P

Phony initial

Use this clue on the envelope, to
show that it is a spy message and
should be handled carefully.

It works like this:

1 Phony initial after first name
means 'invisible message inside'.

2 Phony initial before first
name means 'code message,
open secretly'.

Invisible message indicator

Agree on a certain day of the week
to stand for each of the developers
(powder, heat and wash). Use a
certain time to stand for each of
the places where a message might
be written, such as:

1 pm—Along sides

2 pm—Between lines

3 pm—Back of letter

4 pm—Inside envelope

Testing for secret writing

Take care when testing an intercepted message, or one without an indicator. First hold the paper at an angle to the light, as shown, to check for any telltale glints. Then make your tests in the order shown on the chart.

ORDER OF TESTS
1. USE POWDER TO TEST FOR WAX MESSAGE.
2. USE HEAT TO TEST FOR MILK OR JUICE MESSAGE.
3. USE WASH TO TEST FOR MESSAGE. WRITTEN WITH WATER.

POWDER   WASH

HEAT

Have all your materials ready so you can quickly run through the tests. For the powder you can use chalk scrapings, powdered coffee, dry mustard, red pepper or even fine earth.

To make a wash, mix equal parts of water and ink (or watery paint). For a heat developer, you can use a light bulb instead of an oven. Hold the paper close, moving it so it does not scorch.

Secret code ring

This is an easy way to set up a secret communication link with your Contacts. Use the different signs on the ring to pass messages without making Enemy agents suspicious.

Wear the ring with one or two of the signs showing on top of your finger when you want to pass a message. Try to look casual when you change the tubes or move the ring from one finger to another.

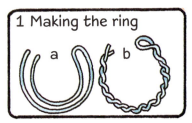

Cut a piece of fuse wire long enough to make a double ring around your middle finger (a). Twist the two strands of wire tightly together (b).

Make four tiny tubes of rolled-up paper. Paint one red, one blue, one yellow and one green (c). Slip them over one end of the wire and join up the ends of the ring (d).

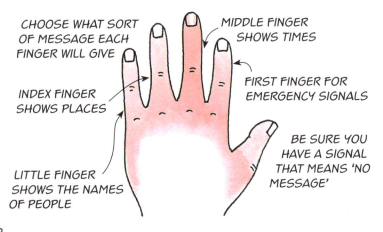

CHOOSE WHAT SORT OF MESSAGE EACH FINGER WILL GIVE

MIDDLE FINGER SHOWS TIMES

INDEX FINGER SHOWS PLACES

FIRST FINGER FOR EMERGENCY SIGNALS

LITTLE FINGER SHOWS THE NAMES OF PEOPLE

BE SURE YOU HAVE A SIGNAL THAT MEANS 'NO MESSAGE'

Secret code book

Keep a secret code book to remind you what the different shades on each finger mean. In case the Enemy finds your code book, you can put the words in code or initials just to remind you.

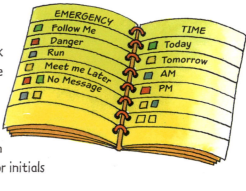

1 Enemy alert

The Good Spy is waiting for a secret meeting with her Contact when an Enemy Spy arrives.

2

Now the Contact approaches. How can the Good Spy stop him from revealing his identity?

3

The Good Spy moves the code ring to her first finger with red showing. This means DANGER.

4

The Contact sees the warning signal and walks straight on, unsuspected by the Enemy agent.

Emergency signals

Here are some more simple codes to help you pass secret messages to your Contacts. Keep a secret code book for these codes too, like the one on the previous page—then you won't forget what the different signs mean.

Make up your own order code to pass messages to a Contact at a conference or meeting. Just arrange your pencils, pens, ruler and other things in a different order along your desk.

Face code

DANGER   KEEP AWAY   MEET ME LATER

This simple face code is probably the easiest one of all to use in an emergency. Just sit with your first finger on, or pointing to, different

Pencil code set

You need an ordinary matchbox, three pencils of different shades and a rubber band.

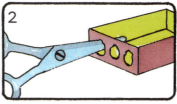

Make three holes, like this, in the end of the matchbox tray, big enough for the pencils.

Put the rubber band around the tray, to stop it from slipping. Push the tray into the box.

Arrange the pencils in a code order to pass a message. Put the set in your top pocket.

parts of your face to pass secret messages. Rest your head on your hand and sit still until your Contact notices your signals.

41

Newspaper messages

Newspapers, magazines and comics are very useful for passing secret messages. You can drop one with a message inside almost anywhere without arousing suspicion. The message is so secret that only a Contact who has been tipped off will find it.

Use one of these two ways of writing the message and leave the newspaper, magazine or comic where people usually read them. You can drop it in a bin, leave it on the seat of a train or bus, or on the table in a cafe. But your Contact must be ready to pick it up, or an Enemy agent or an innocent passerby may get there first.

Crossword messages

Many newspapers and magazines have a crossword in them. Fill in the blank squares with the message. Write downwards only. Fill the other squares with any random letters to complete the crossword.

Leave the paper for your Contact to collect. No one bothers to look at a crossword that has already been filled in, so this is a good way to pass an urgent message.

1 Pinhole messages

On the front page of a newspaper you'll find the date. Prick a small hole with a pin over one number of the date. This will tell your Contact which page you have marked with the secret message.

Turn to that page of the newspaper. Use the pin to prick holes over the letters as you spell out the message. Prick a hole in the space between the printed words to show the end of a message word.

To read the message, fold the newspaper so that the page with the message has no other pages behind it. Hold it up to the light. You can then see the pinholes and read the letters at the same time.

Rehearse reading pinhole messages in secret. Then you will be able to read them while being watched, but without arousing the suspicions of the person who is watching you.

Planning a rendezvous

Members of a Good Spy Ring need many emergency plans for meeting at a secret Rendezvous and passing messages. These plans can have code names, such as RP (Rendezvous Plan) A, B or C. A Spy can then send a very short message to his Contact, just saying 'RP Q' or 'RP Y'. Then they meet at the Rendezvous, pretending not to know each other, and pass a written message which is not in code. Here are ways to pass messages under the eyes of a watchful Enemy.

Meet by a notice board. Stand near the Contact, pretending to make notes. Ask to borrow a pen from the 'stranger'.

Give back another pen, which looks the same. The message is hidden inside the barrel or rolled up in the cap.

Meet at a public building or tourist office. Pretend not to know each other. The Contact has a map.

The Spy asks to borrow the map. He slides out the message hidden inside and gives back the map.

A Spy meets his Contact sitting on a park bench. They do not speak. The Spy reads his newspaper.

The Spy folds up his paper, puts it down and walks away. The Contact has to watch the Enemy.

She picks up the paper and reads it for a while. Then she leaves, carrying the newspaper.

Inside the newspaper is a long message. A piece of tape on one corner stops it from slipping out.

A Spy and her Contact carry similar bags with messages. They swap them as they pass.

Two spies hang up their hats, with messages inside, in a cafe. As they go, they take each other's hats.

Secret teamwork

You can use these codes to pass information secretly to your Contacts when there are other people or Enemy agents near.

You can also use them to show your powers of thought-reading at a party. While you are out of the room, the others choose an object or a person or a number. When you come back you will be able to name it correctly, because your partner has used one of these codes to give you the information.

This and that

For this trick, leave the room while the others choose an object. Your partner puts it among some other objects set out in two groups (or lines). Secretly, you have agreed that one group is called 'This' and the other 'That'.

When you return, your partner points to these things one by one,

asking 'Is it this one?' or 'Is it that one?' When he uses the word 'This' for things in the 'This' line or 'That' for things in the 'That' line, you answer 'No'.

But as soon as he uses the word 'This' for an object in a 'That' line, or 'That' for something in a 'This' line, you know it is the right one.

Name code

Here is another trick that doesn't need any preparation — just an agreement between you and your partner.

Your audience will be baffled when you pick out a person or an object that they have chosen, without your partner even asking you any questions. You can just walk in and tell them which one it is. Or you could even let one of the audience ask you questions.

When you are out of the room, your partner arranges the audience in a line, or puts some things in a line. All the things can be the same — such as ten oranges — which will make the trick seem even more amazing.

Then the audience chooses one of them. When they are ready, your partner tells you secretly which is the chosen person or thing. He does this by the position of your name in his words.

If he calls out 'Peter, you can come in now', your name is the first word. You know the chosen person or thing is in the first position. If he calls out 'We are ready now, Peter', the word 'Peter' is the fifth word. You know that the chosen person or object is in the fifth position.

To make the trick look even better, pretend you are getting secret messages from the different objects.

More secret teamwork

Secret numbers

This trick uses an easy number code known only to you and your partner. You can make your audience believe you can read a certain number in his or her mind.

When you are out of the room, your partner tells the audience to choose a number — for example 629. He then tells them he will say a list of numbers to you, but that when he comes to 629, you will know it is the chosen number.

When you come back into the room, but before he starts to say numbers to you, he decides when to say 629. If, for example, he decides to say it fifth, the trick is that the total of the numbers of the first one he says, add up to 5.

His first question might be 'Is it 32?' Your answer would be 'No'. But his question will have told you that the chosen number is fifth, because 32 is made up of 3 and 2, which add up to 5. His first number could also have been 23 or 14 or 41, because the two numbers of each also add up to 5. If he decides to say the chosen number seventh, then the total of the numbers of the first one must add up to 7.

It doesn't matter what the next three numbers are — because you know that none of them are the chosen one. It makes it more mysterious if he uses big numbers. For example, 32, 4619, 824, 99 and then 629.

THE SPOTS AREN'T HERE - THEY SHOW IMAGINARY POSITIONS

Pattern codes

To do this trick, your partner lays out five cards or mats or books in a row. You have to guess which one they have chosen. The secret of the code is that each one has five imaginary positions on it, like this:

1 2 3 4 5

While you are out of the room, the audience picks one of them. When you come back, your partner points to any one of them and says 'Is it this one?' Your answer will be 'No' but the position where he touches it will tell you which the chosen card or mat or book is. So if he touches it in the middle, it means the chosen one is third; or if he touches it in the bottom right hand corner, it means the

chosen one is fifth in the row.

You can also do this trick with nine positions:

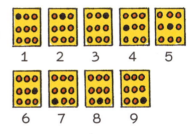

1 2 3 4 5

6 7 8 9

Then you can use nine objects in a row.

The code can also be used for passing secret messages. For example, you could hold your thumb on position three when you hand a book to a Contact, or you could scratch a certain part of the back of your hand. This might mean, 'Enemy alert—follow me when I leave'.

49

Morse messages

Morse code is useful for flashing messages in the dark and tapping them out in daylight. Make two quick taps for a dot and four for a dash.

Flash messages with a flashlight. Some have a button to press.

Draw the curtains in a room and flip up the edge of one to flash.

Draw back the curtains in a room with the light on. Cover the light with your hat to flash the code.

In a room with a roller blind, pull it halfway down for a dot and all the way for a dash.

Morse code

A ● ▬		H ●●●●
B ▬ ●●●		I ●●
C ▬ ● ▬ ●		J ● ▬ ▬ ▬
D ▬ ●●		K ▬ ● ▬
E ●		L ● ▬ ●●
F ●● ▬ ●		M ▬ ▬
G ▬ ▬ ●		N ▬ ●

Count one slowly for a flash dot and two slowly for a flash dash. Make sure your Contact knows when to watch or listen.

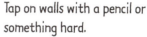
Tapped messages

Tap on water pipes or radiators in a building.

Tap on walls with a pencil or something hard.

Tap on railings. Your Contact will have to put his ear against them.

Tap the ground. Your Contact listens at the end of his stick.

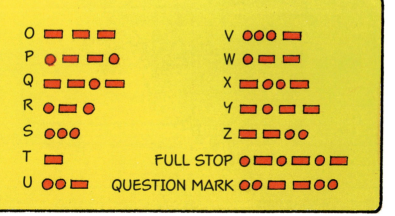

O ▬ ▬ ▬	V ●●● ▬
P ● ▬ ▬ ●	W ● ▬ ▬
Q ▬ ▬ ● ▬	X ▬ ●● ▬
R ● ▬ ●	Y ▬ ● ▬ ▬
S ●●●	Z ▬ ▬ ●●
T ▬	
U ●● ▬	

FULL STOP ● ▬ ● ▬ ● ▬

QUESTION MARK ●● ▬ ▬ ●●

Pocket spy kit

Here is how to fit all your basic spy equipment into a matchbox. It holds an invisible writing kit, hollow twig disguise, code card, and all you need for signpost signals.

Make three mini-pens: a pencil for code messages, a bit of white crayon or candle for wax writing and chalk for signpost signals and wax developing. The next pages show how to make dividers and a lifting string for fast action in emergencies.

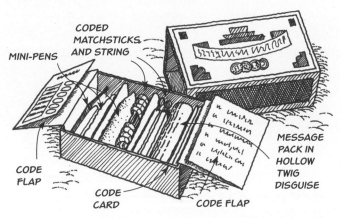

MINI-PENS

CODED MATCHSTICKS AND STRING

CODE FLAP

CODE CARD

CODE FLAP

MESSAGE PACK IN HOLLOW TWIG DISGUISE

For the container, you will need:

1. A matchbox

2. Stiff paper or thin cardboard (a postcard is good)

3. Scissors and a pencil

4. Strong glue and sticky tape

5. Needle and thread for the lifter (shown on the next pages)

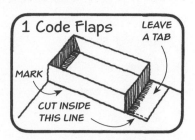

1 Code Flaps   LEAVE A TAB

MARK

CUT INSIDE THIS LINE

Draw around the matchbox on cardboard, leaving a bit extra. Cut two strips of cardboard, slightly narrower than this.

Matchstick holder

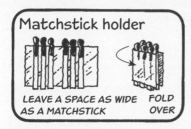

LEAVE A SPACE AS WIDE AS A MATCHSTICK   FOLD OVER

Lay six coded matchsticks (broken to size) on a bit of sticky tape, leaving a space in the middle. Fold the strip as shown.

String holder

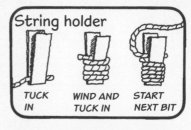

TUCK IN   WIND AND TUCK IN   START NEXT BIT

Fold a strip of cardboard, cut to fit inside the box. Tuck the end of the string into the fold. Wind it around and tuck in the other end.

Making mini-pens

PRESS HARD

ROLL PENCIL

To cut down a pencil, chalk or bit of candle, saw around with a knife to make a deep groove. Then you can break it along the groove.

Message pack

Cut strips of paper a bit narrower than the tray. Wind tightly round a matchstick, one by one. Tuck into a hollow twig.

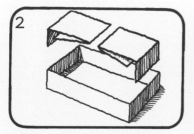

Fold the strips like this, so that the folded flaps will fit together in the tray when you close the box. Bend down the tabs and trim.

WRITE ON THESE BITS

GLUE IN THE TABS HERE

Write the codes on one flap and the meanings on the other. Once you have done this, you then glue the tabs into the tray.

53

Quick action lifter

Fix a secret thread inside your spy kit, as shown below. Then you can make the contents pop up when you need them. Measure carefully—it will save you valuable time when you are in action.

You can disguise the kit to look like part of a stamp collection in case you are stopped and searched by the Enemy.

When you pull the loop, a thread in the tray lifts up the things inside.

1 Making the lifter

MARK TWICE THE DEPTH

CUT OUT A BIT NARROWER

Measure and cut out three strips of thin cardboard. Make each a bit narrower than the tray and about twice as long as it is deep.

2

LEAVE SOME SPACE ABOVE

FOLD AND CHECK

Fold each strip like this and check that it fits well into the tray. Dab glue inside and press tightly. Leave to dry.

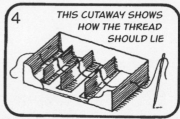

Poke a threaded needle through the top of one strip. Knot it as shown. Glue this strip down across the middle of the tray.

Glue the other pieces on either side. Poke the thread through the ends of the tray. Pull it tight to lie flat in each compartment.

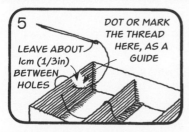

At each end, push the threaded needle back into the tray, like this. Make a mark on the thread where it comes out.

Make a knot in the thread just where the dot is. Cut off the rest. Pull the thread back in again and pack in your equipment on top.

1 Disguising the box

Cut a piece of cardboard a bit longer and narrower than the tray. Fold down the ends so that it fits just over the tray.

Glue a few old stamps to the cardboard, making sure they overlap, like this. Staple or sew on one stamp to use as the lifter.

Message scrambler

You can use this sort of code for sending secret messages up to 24 letters long. You can choose any Keyword and use one of the Routes explained below. If the Enemy Spies crack your code, make up a new Keyword and choose a different Route.

Keywords

Your Keyword can be any word in which none of the letters appears more than once. But it is easier to use words which have four, five or six letters in them. Try the following examples: ZEBRAS, WREN, GHOST, LAMB, SPIDER, SHADOW, BAKER or CAKE.

Routes

The Route is the direction in which you write out the words of your message underneath or beside your Keyword.

Here are some examples of different Routes — follow the letters of the alphabet to see how each one goes.

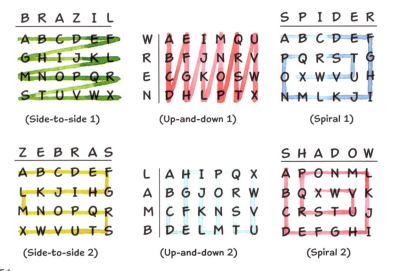

(Side-to-side 1)

(Up-and-down 1)

(Spiral 1)

(Side-to-side 2)

(Up-and-down 2)

(Spiral 2)

56

Sending a message

When you want to send a message, first make sure that you and the person who will receive it are using the same Keyword and the same Route.

So if the message you want to send is SPY ZERO SIX MUST ACT QUICKLY, and you decide to use Keyword BRAZIL and route SIDE TO SIDE 1 — you set your message out like this:

B R A Z I L
S P Y Z E R
O S I X M U
S T A C T Q
U I C K L Y

Then, to put the message into code, you read off the new coded words in vertical lines, in the alphabetical order of the Keyword. So the letters under A of BRAZIL are the first coded word, and the letters under Z of BRAZIL are the last. Now your message in code reads YIAC SOSU EMTL RUQY PSTI ZXCK.

If there are not enough letters in the message you want to send, in order to fill the spaces under your Keyword you must fill up the empty spaces with the letter X.

Receiving a message

When you receive a message, you do exactly the opposite to the sender. For example, if you receive the following message — OTOQ LHNA CKTH CGIT GOTO OXIS — and you are using Keyword SHADOW and Route SPIRAL 2, you first write down the Keyword — SHADOW.

Then you write down the coded message like this: OTOQ, under the A of SHADOW, LHNA under the D, CKTH under the H, CGIT under the

O, GOTO under the S, and OXIS under the W. So now the coded message will look like this.

S H A D O W
G C O L C O
O K T H G X
T T O N I I
O H Q A T S

Then you simply read off the actual message by following Route SPIRAL 2.

Keyword alphabet codes

You can make a good code by swapping each of
your message letters with the matching letter in a
Keyword alphabet. Some examples are shown
below. Notice that each begins with a word or
phrase in which no letter is repeated. This is the
Keyword. The rest of the alphabet follows.

Plain alphabets	Keyword alphabets					
A	B	C	M	M	I	P
B	E	A	Y	I	M	U
C	W	R	O	S	P	R
D	A	E	L	F	O	C
E	T	F	D	O	R	H
F	C	U	A	R	T	A
G	H	L	U	T	A	S
H	F	S	N	U	N	I
I	U	P	T	N	C	N
J	L	Y	S	E	E	G
K	D	B	B	A	B	B
L	G	D	C	B	D	D
M	I	G	E	C	F	E
N	J	H	F	D	G	F
O	K	I	G	G	H	J
P	M	J	H	H	J	K
Q	N	K	I	J	K	L
R	O	M	J	K	L	M
S	P	N	K	L	Q	O
T	Q	O	P	P	S	Q
U	R	Q	Q	Q	U	T
V	S	T	R	V	V	V
W	V	V	V	W	W	W
X	X	W	W	X	X	X
Y	Y	X	X	Y	Y	Y
Z	Z	Z	Z	Z	Z	Z

Instant codes

These instant codes are useful for sending written messages in code. In each one, a different shape stands for a letter of the alphabet.

   On the next two pages are four instant codes. You can either learn them or use the pages for encoding and decoding your secret messages. You can also copy them and change the order of the letters to make the code more secret. Give a copy to your Contact so he or she knows the code.

Pig-pen code

This looks very strange but it is easy to use. A line shape, or a shape and a dot, stands for each letter of the alphabet. Here is a message in code.

Semaphore

Semaphore is usually signalled with flags. Here you use the same positions of the flags but written like the hands of a clock.

Morse code

This is usually written as dots and dashes. Tall peaks stand for dashes and short ones for dots. A line means the end of a letter. A line break is the end of a word.

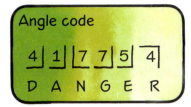

Angle code

In this code, a line shape with a number stands for the letters. Starting at the beginning of the alphabet, a shape is numbered 1 to 7. Then the shape is changed.

More instant codes

PLAIN	PIG-PEN	MORSE	SEMAPHORE	ANGLE
A				
B				
C				
D				
E				
F				
G				
H				
I				
J				
K				
L				
M				

PLAIN	PIG-PEN	MORSE	SEMAPHORE	ANGLE
N	⊡	/\/\	◓	⌐7
O	⊡	/\/\/\	◴	⌐1
P	⌐·	/\/\/\	◔	⌐2
Q	⌐·⌐	/\/\/\	◷	⌐3
R	⌐·	/\/\	⊖	⌐4
S	V	/\/\/\	◠	⌐5
T	>	/\	◔	⌐6
U	<	/\/\	◔	⌐7
V	/\	/\/\/\	◐	⌐1
W	·/\·	/\/\	◔	⌐2
X	·>	/\/\/\	◐	⌐3
Y	<·	/\/\/\	◔	⌐4
Z	/\·	/\/\/\	◔	⌐5

61

Decoding practice

Decode these messages (written in instant codes) to get a glimpse at the spy's world of danger and intrigue . . .

1 From Agent ZK to Agent YW

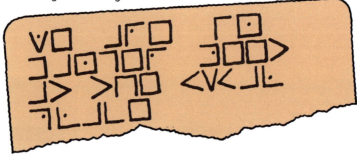

2 From Agent YW to Agent ZK

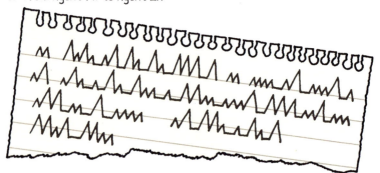

3 From Agent ZK to Agent YW

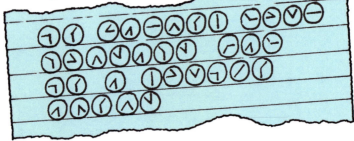

4   From Agent YW to Agent ZK

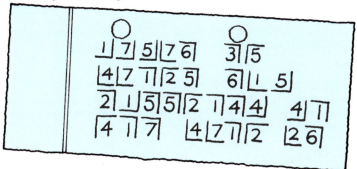

5   From Agent ZK to Agent YW

Answers

These are the decoded messages:

1   We are in danger — meet at the usual place.

2   I cannot. I have a rendezvous with Agent QZ.

3   Be warned — your contact may be a double-agent.

4   Agent QZ knows the password. Do you know it?

5   Send no more messages.

The fact that Agent ZK does not show the password may look suspicious — actually he himself is a double-agent. That is why he is trying to prevent Agent YW from meeting Agent QZ. Agent QZ has blown his cover (discovered his true identity).

Test your observation

To become a really Good Spy, you must train yourself to notice even the smallest details of every situation. Test your powers of observation, and then your friends' by covering up the right-

hand page and looking carefully at the left-hand page only. Then cover this up and see how many things you can see that are different on the right-hand page. There are 20. Can you spot them all?

Who stole the secret plans?

One foggy afternoon an Enemy agent breaks into a top security building and steals some secret plans. Several people see him hurrying away.

A policeman stated that the suspect was wearing dark glasses and had three buttons on his coat.

A little boy said he was carrying a stick in his left hand.

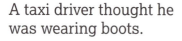

An old lady thought the suspect had a bald head and a briefcase. An old man reported that he was wearing a spotted tie.

A taxi driver thought he was wearing boots.

The policeman, the old man and the lady were right. The little boy and the taxi driver were wrong. Which picture shows the guilty spy?

Answer

The spy who stole the documents is number 9. He is wearing shoes, dark glasses and a spotted tie, has a bald head and three buttons on his coat. He is carrying a briefcase, and a stick in his right hand.

Stalking, tracking and shadowing

A Good Spy is able to follow his Quarry — the person he is following — through town or countryside, without being noticed. But he has to change his tactics depending on the route taken by the Quarry. Here are some of the main skills you will need to be a Good Spy.

Stalking

WEAR CLOTHES THAT MATCH YOUR SURROUNDINGS

STICK CLOSE TO COVER (THINGS THAT HIDE YOU OR BLEND WITH YOUR SHAPE)

QUARRY

WEAR SOFT SOLED SHOES

In the country, creep after your Quarry as you would follow a wild animal. Move quietly and stay hidden as much as possible. This is called stalking. Your stalking skills will help you to get close enough to watch wild creatures too. This is good practice.

Your clothes should blend into your surroundings and match the main shades of the landscape. Mixtures of shades, such as tan, green and brown, are the best. Choose the ones that go with the type of country where you are stalking your Quarry.

Tracking

QUARRY

WATCH FOR SIGNS
THAT SHOW WHERE YOUR
QUARRY HAS GONE

If you lose your Quarry, you will have to look for clues to find which
way he or she has gone and follow them. This is called tracking.

Shadowing

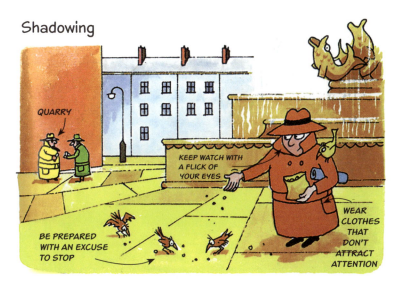

QUARRY

KEEP WATCH WITH
A FLICK OF
YOUR EYES

BE PREPARED
WITH AN EXCUSE
TO STOP

WEAR
CLOTHES
THAT
DON'T
ATTRACT
ATTENTION

In a town, you must be able to merge with the background so that
your Quarry never notices you. You have to follow him at all times
without appearing to watch him. This is called shadowing. There are
lots of tricks to learn for this.

How to stalk

When stalking, any noise or movement may give you away. Move silently and smoothly, keeping in the cover of hedges and trees whenever possible. The next few pages show special walks and crawls for different kinds of cover. Try not to make quick movements, even with your head. Swivel your eyes to look around you. Try to be ready to stop and stay still the moment you see danger.

To walk silently, step very lightly putting each foot down flat, then lifting it carefully clear of the ground. Rehearse this by walking on dry twigs, stones and gravel.

Remember that animals have a keen sense of smell. If you are stalking an animal, or if the Enemy Spy has a dog, stay downwind so your scent will be blown away from him. If you are upwind, it will blow your scent towards him and you may be discovered.

Look at this picture to get a few more tips.

Checking the wind

CHILLY SIDE
(UPWIND SIDE)

LEAVES BLOW DOWNWIND

WIND BLOWS THIS WAY

To check wind direction, wet your finger and hold it up. The colder side faces upwind. Another way is to toss some dust, dry leaves or bits of grass up into the air. They will blow downwind.

Never stand or walk on the skyline—everyone will be able to see you.

Keep shiny things out of the Sun's glare. They may attract attention.

When you stop, keep in the shade, but make sure that your shadow does not give you away.

Checking for tracks

When searching the ground for tracks, shield your eyes like this, and look towards the Sun. If there is even a small dent in the ground, the shadow made by the Sun will make it show up more.

Stalker's kit

When you go out stalking, always keep your hands free, and only carry the things you think you will really need in your pockets. Try to be prepared for all situations.

Don't carry your kit in a bag or hang things around your neck. They might catch in bushes or fences or get in your way if you have to crawl. Wear clothes with big pockets and put everything there.

Use your front pockets for flat things, such as a map, notebooks and your camouflage headband. Use your back pockets for any bulky things, such as a flashlight. Then you will not lie on them if you have to crawl along on your stomach.

It is a good idea to take some rations with you in case you get hungry—nuts and raisins are good. Keep them in a small plastic bag with an elastic band twisted around it. Below you can see some other things you might find useful.

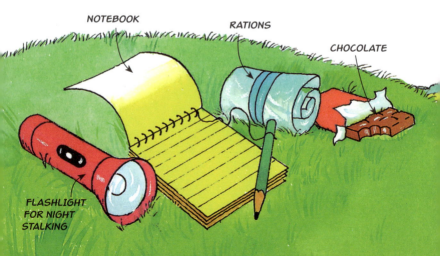

NOTEBOOK

RATIONS

CHOCOLATE

FLASHLIGHT
FOR NIGHT
STALKING

Camouflage headband

Cut a band of material long enough to go around your head, and a piece of cloth tape, about 1m (3ft) long.

THE TAPE TIES AROUND YOUR HEAD

Pin the tape to the band with safety pins — one at each end and four or five more in between them.

Choose bits of twig, leaves or grass to match your surroundings. Push them between the pins, like this.

You can quickly remove or change your camouflage if you enter a different kind of territory.

Try to wear clothes that blend with your surroundings — dull, drab shades are usually best.

They should be old and tough for crawling in, but smooth enough not to catch in spiky bushes.

Stalking walks and crawls

When stalking, use things that can hide you, like walls and bushes. These are called 'cover'. You can use the methods shown below when cover is scarce.

The walk

In good cover, like trees, you can walk upright. But keep your arms still and your hands by your sides.

Feline crawl

Do this crawl on your hands and knees, keeping your back flat and low. At each step lift your foot just clear of the ground.

Never drag your feet. It is important to keep your head down low and try not to bob it up and down.

Seal crawl

Lie flat on your stomach with your legs together and straight, and your toes turned out to keep your heels low. Reach out, pull with your forearms and push with your toes to move forward.

The crouch

Near low cover, you may have to crouch to keep your head down. Hold your thighs to help you keep in the crouch position and stay balanced. Don't shuffle. Lift your feet off the ground with each step.

Flat feline crawl

Lie slightly sideways, one leg straight and the other bent so the inside of the knee touches the ground.

Move by pressing on your forearms and bent knee to raise your body slightly and push it forward.

Using cover

The spy in the black hat will easily be seen. The one in the brown hat is making good use of cover. When peering around a wall or tree, remember — one eye is enough. This hides the shape of your head.

Stalking practice

All these games will help you rehearse stalking. For the outdoor game shown right, you need a good stalking area. Look for an area with bushes, dips in the land, long grass or trees to use as cover. This game will help you learn to use cover, to move quietly and to wait and watch without being seen.

Use the indoor games below to train yourself to listen for tiny sounds, to move around silently and stay in one spot without moving.

Clock hunt

This game teaches you to use your ears, as well as your eyes. Any number of people can play. One person hides a clock with a loud tick somewhere in a room, while the others wait outside. These players then have one minute to discover where the clock is hidden, moving nothing.

Steal the plans

For this game you need at least three players. Put some folded papers under a chair in the middle of the room. One person is the guard. He sits on the chair blindfolded, with a rolled-up newspaper as a weapon. The others sit on the floor. One by one, they try to steal the papers without being heard or hit by the guard. If a player steals the treasure he becomes the next guard. If he is hit, he loses his turn.

Beat the guards

You need at least four players for this. Two stand blindfolded on either side of an open door. One by one, the others try to creep from the opposite wall through the door. If a guard hears a player, he puts out his arm. If the player is touched he goes back to the wall. A player who gets past becomes a guard.

Hide and stalk

You need two players — Stalker and Quarry. If there is a third person, he or she can take the loser's place after each round. Stalker and Quarry try to spot each other without being spotted.

Choose something like a tree trunk or big stone as your base. The Stalker waits here while the Quarry runs off about 100m (110yds) to hide. He or she can go further if cover is scarce, but must stay within earshot. When they are hidden, they shout 'Ready!' Then the stalker shouts 'Ready!' and begins to stalk their Quarry.

The first one to spot the other calls their name and says 'You're spotted!' The loser is the Stalker for the next round. To win the game, you have to make three spottings in a row.

When you are the Quarry, try hiding close to base in order to fool the Stalker. Wait a bit before you call 'Ready!', to make them think you are further away. Stay quiet until you hear them go past, then creep out behind them.

When you are the Stalker, listen carefully to your Quarry's shout. Try to work out where the sound is coming from, and how far away it is. Try circling around the spot where your Quarry might be hiding to take them by surprise. But remember they can move around as well. Stop from time to time to listen for telltale noises.

Training course

A good Stalker can move silently anywhere, even through undergrowth and across stony ground. Here are some ideas for a training course.

Set it up somewhere secret with other Good Spies. Take turns to be the Trainer. The Trainer stands with his back to the course while the others, one by one, try to creep up and touch him. Each time he hears a noise, he calls out and the Stalker loses a point. See who loses the fewest points while stalking.

STONES
MARK
START

Lay planks across some bricks. Scatter stones on them. Each Stalker tries to walk on them without rattling the stones.

Tie a string between two sticks, like this. Hang pairs of metal lids from it, so low you have to flatten yourself to creep under.

Arrange some tin cans so that the Stalkers must move very carefully to walk past them. Stack the cans or put a few stones in them so they rattle if knocked.

Then cover stretches of ground with things that crunch or rustle, like gravel, twigs, dry leaves or newspaper.

TRAINER

1 Clanging lids

STICKY TAPE

2

CLANG!

Tie a piece of string around each lid. Knot it and hold it in place with bits of sticky tape.

Hang the lids on the string, quite close together. Then they will clatter if one of them is touched.

Searchlight

This game tests your skill at moving silently in the dark and listening for noises. You can play it in an open area with any number of people. One person is the warder. He or she carries a flashlight. The rest are prisoners who try to creep from the start line to the safety line without the warder spotting them. The first prisoner to reach the safety line is the winner, who becomes the next warder. Mark the ground with a start line and a safety line.

When the warder shouts 'Ready!' the prisoners begin creeping to safety. If the warder hears a noise, he points the unlit flashlight to where he thinks the prisoner is, and shouts 'Halt!' Nobody moves. Then he turns on the light. Any prisoner who is caught in the light must go back ten paces, counting out loud. The warder points the light upwards to show that everyone else must stay still. When he switches the light off, the game goes on.

If no one is caught in the light, the warder has made a false challenge and must switch off the light. If he makes three false challenges, he loses the game and the prisoner nearest to the safety line becomes the warder.

STONES MARK
THE START LINE

STONES MARK
THE SAFETY LINE

If it is not dark enough, the warder can use a blindfold and look over it after he makes a challenge. Or else the warder can be blindfolded and have an assistant who stands beside him. When the warder makes a challenge, the assistant shouts out 'True!' or 'False!' but is not allowed to help the warder spot the prisoner. If the prisoner wins, he or she becomes the assistant, and the assistant becomes the warder. If the warder and assistant win, they swap places for the next game.

Tracking gadgets

Here are two useful gadgets to help your tracking skills. Try them either during the day or at night.

Drag a Whifflepoof by the string. It works well on grass. Make a continuous track or it will be difficult to follow. The tracks show up well at night. If you shine a flashlight along them, you can see which way they go. They will look darker than the rest of the grass coming towards you and lighter going away.

Use the Tracking Stick like a walking stick. Make a track every few steps on soft, wet ground or on wet sand.

Tracking stick

You will need:
1. A can lid with a rim
2. An old broom handle or thick walking stick
3. A nail, and screw about 3cm (1in) long
4. Hammer and screwdriver
5. Pliers

GRIP AND TWIST

1. Grip the lid with the pliers and twist them to make a kink in the rim.
2. Hammer the nail into the lid to make a hole. Then use it to start a hole in the stick. Get someone to hold the stick while you screw on the lid.

SCREW IN LIKE THIS

Whifflepoof

You will need:

1. A small log
2. Some big nails
3. A hammer
4. A piece of cord or thick string, about 3m (10ft) long

Ask someone to hold the log down firmly on its side for you. Hammer nails all around it. Hammer each one about halfway in. Hammer two more nails almost all the way into one end of the log, one on each side. Tie one end of the cord or string around each of these nails.

Covering your tracks

When you are out in the country, take care not to leave obvious tracks yourself, in case you too are being followed. You should be safe if you stick mainly to hard or stony ground, short grass or fallen leaves.

But just in case your pursuer is an experienced tracker, here are some extra tricks that may hold him up and throw him off your track.

Walk on the hard made-up part of roads, not along the soft edges, and try to avoid sandy paths.

To cross a stream, find stepping stones. Do not get wet feet in case you leave damp footprints.

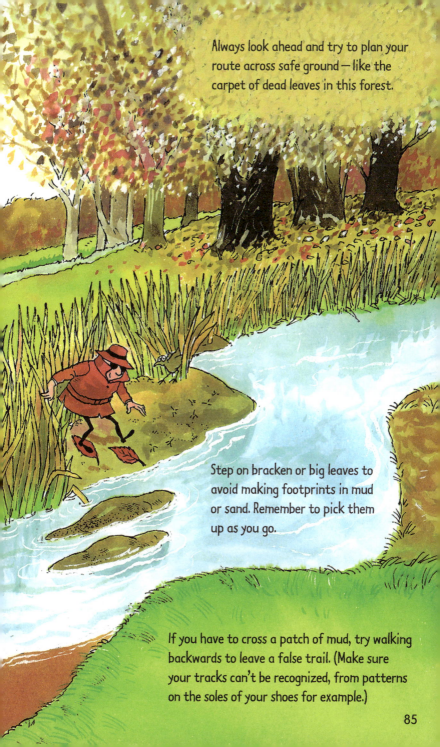

Always look ahead and try to plan your route across safe ground — like the carpet of dead leaves in this forest.

Step on bracken or big leaves to avoid making footprints in mud or sand. Remember to pick them up as you go.

If you have to cross a patch of mud, try walking backwards to leave a false trail. (Make sure your tracks can't be recognized, from patterns on the soles of your shoes for example.)

Using landmarks

If ever you find yourself coming into territory you do not know, look out for landmarks that will help you to find your way back again. Anything that stands out obviously will do, so long as it can't move. It must still be there when you want to come back.

In towns, use landmarks such as churches and shops. In the country, look for stiles, gates, farmhouses, stone walls and lone trees.

Memorize things so that you recognize them on the way back. Here are some things to look for.

RADIO OR TV MAST

WIND PUMP

ELECTRICITY PYLONS

OBELISK

RAILWAY LINE

RESERVOIR

WATERFALL

LONE ROCK

MILESTONE

BRIDGE

RIVER (NOTICE ANY TWISTS AND BENDS)

POND

LONE TREE

STILE

STEPPING STONES

SCARECROW

WARNING

Wherever you are — in the town or country — remember to look back from time to time, especially before you change direction. This will help you to recognize your route on the way back.

Remember that things can look very different when you are going in the other direction — you are seeing the other side of them. The things you noted will also be on the other side. Where you turned left on the way out, you will have to turn right coming back.

RUINS

WINDMILL

CROSS

CLUSTER OF HOUSES

CHURCH

GATE

WEATHER VANE

GOLF COURSE

BEEHIVES

BARN

87

How to shadow

When you are shadowing someone, follow them closely enough not to lose contact, but not so closely that you make them suspicious. Glance at them quickly from time to time, but don't stare. Try looking up and down the street as though you are expecting a friend and quickly note where your Quarry is.

Be careful not to stop and start when your Quarry does—they will be sure to notice. When they stop, walk on at the same pace, even if you have to pass them. Then make some excuse to stop and wait until they come past, then you can begin to follow again.

Always keep a sharp look-out when your Quarry starts getting close to a corner.

If you are not looking, they may suddenly be out of sight before you realize.

Good Spies learn to use their eyes without moving their heads—like this.

If you can see your Quarry's reflection, it means they can also see yours.

Be prepared before you go out, with lots of different excuses for stopping. You must vary your tactics because your Quarry will be sure to notice if you use the same excuse several times. Look in shop windows or ask someone for directions.

If there is a lot of traffic, pretend to be waiting to cross the road. When your Quarry moves on, don't follow them right away, but keep them in sight. If you suspect they are watching you in the reflection of a window, try the window check shown below.

When you hurry after them, slow down again before you reach the corner.

Saunter around it casually. If the Quarry really is a spy, they may be bluffing too.

To see if they are watching you, move to one side so they cannot see your reflection.

If they are suspicious, they will move to try to catch sight of your reflection again.

Shadow's kit

When you are out on a secret mission trailing a Quarry, it is vital that the Quarry does not suspect what you are doing. It is best to wear ordinary clothes so you won't be noticed in a crowd. But, in case you are spotted, it is a good idea to have a quick disguise kit to change into. Keep it in a bag which you can stuff into your pocket afterwards.

Try carrying another sweater or jacket with you, or putting on a hat or scarf so that you look a different shape from a distance. Wear soft-soled shoes so that you can walk quietly and run fast if you need to.

It may be useful to carry a notebook to keep a record of your Quarry's movements and any suspicious activities. You may also want to take down information such as car numbers, train times or descriptions. If you have a street map, you can mark the route your suspect takes, follow them without getting lost, and see how you can cut corners.

1 Doorway quick change

If you think your Quarry has spotted you . . .

2

. . . make a quick obvious change in your looks.

1 Newspaper trick

2

If you want an excuse to stop and spy, when your Quarry stops, carry a newspaper, map or comic.

But be very careful. Lower it just enough to peek over the top, without staring obviously.

1 Pocket book trick

2

Use this double mirror to spy over your shoulder. Move it carefully to get the view you want.

You can camouflage it as a diary, as shown below. Or just slip it inside a book or comic.

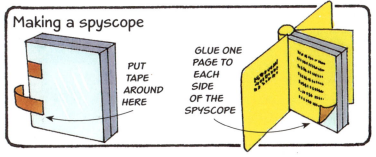

Making a spyscope

PUT TAPE AROUND HERE

GLUE ONE PAGE TO EACH SIDE OF THE SPYSCOPE

Tape two small mirrors together on one side. Make sure you can open and close them easily.

Tear all but the first and last pages from an old diary. Slip the mirror between these pages.

Shaking off a tail

Remember that Enemy Spies might try to shadow you too, so try to think about what they might do, and how you could avoid being followed or 'tailed'. Follow the spy in the brown hat around the picture, and see how he shakes off the Enemy Spies – the ones wearing blue coats.

Use reflections in shop or car windows to see if you are being followed.

To cross a street where you might be spotted, wait until you can be shielded by other people.

Planning a route

If you want to keep your destination secret, it is very important to plan your route carefully. Here are some useful tips:

1. Do not approach your destination by a direct route. Use a zigzag or roundabout path.

2. Vary your route – do not go the same way every time.

3. Do not walk fast – this may alert the Enemy. Stroll along looking at buildings and read notices as if you are out for a walk.

Look for side streets with turnings in easy reach. Dodge in when your tail's view is blocked.

Once you are out of sight of your tail, avoid long stretches of street until you are safely clear.

Quick change trick

Stop and gaze into a shop window. Often your tail will stop too. Then turn and walk towards him.

If your tail walks away, you can disappear down a side street while his back is turned.

Catch the spy

This is an outdoors spying game for two teams. One team (the Spy Ring) is made up of Couriers plus a Spy. The other team are Spycatchers.

Each Courier tries to deliver a message (a rolled-up newspaper) to the Spy at a secret Rendezvous, and then protect him as he delivers the message to a Control spot.

Each Spycatcher tries to discover the secret Rendezvous by shadowing one of the Couriers. He then tries to arrest the Spy as the Spy carries all the messages to a Control spot.

How to play the game:

1. Together, the teams choose starting points and two Controls as on the map. Chalk a large circle on the ground at each Control.

2. The Spy Ring meets secretly to choose a Rendezvous. The Spy has a 3-minute start to get there. He chalks another circle at the Rendezvous. (The Spy is always safe when standing inside a chalk circle.)

3. Then the Couriers wave to the Spycatchers and make for the Rendezvous.

4. The Spycatchers follow as secretly as possible, so as not to be arrested (touched by a Courier). If arrested, they must freeze until the Courier is out of sight.

5. The Spy stays at the Rendezvous until he has all the messages. (The Couriers can scout around to see which Control might be safest.) Then the Spy makes for one of the Controls, guarded by the Couriers.

6. If the Spy is arrested with his messages, the Spycatchers have won. If he reaches a Control safely, the Spy Ring has won.

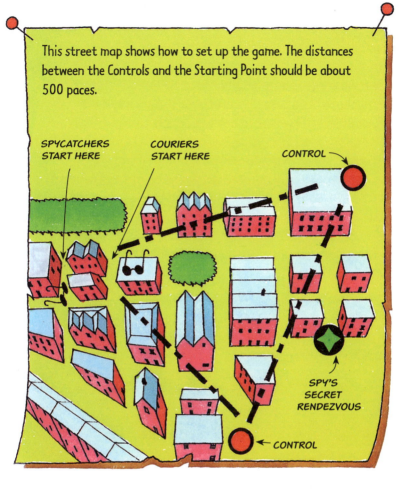

This street map shows how to set up the game. The distances between the Controls and the Starting Point should be about 500 paces.

SPYCATCHERS START HERE

COURIERS START HERE

CONTROL

SPY'S SECRET RENDEZVOUS

CONTROL

Courier arrest

SPY-CATCHER

COURIER

A Courier cannot be arrested. He can arrest a Spycatcher by touching him.

Spycatcher arrest

SPY

SPYCATCHER

To arrest the Spy, a Spycatcher must touch him before being touched by a Courier.

95

Trail signs

Here are some special signs you can use to show a contact where you have gone. They may be useful if you have left your hideout to stalk Enemy Spies.

Make signs with twigs, stones or deep scratches in the ground. They should be just big enough for a careful observer to see them. Put them in sheltered places or at the side of your path so they will not be disturbed by other walkers. Be sure that you are not watched while you are laying the trail.

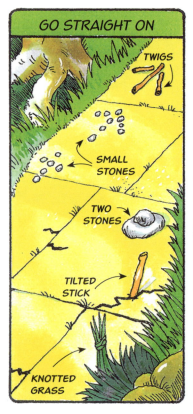

GO STRAIGHT ON

TWIGS

SMALL STONES

TWO STONES

TILTED STICK

KNOTTED GRASS

DO NOT GO THIS WAY

CROSSED TWIGS

BROKEN TWIGS

ROW OF STONES

SMALL STONES

TWIGS

Study the pictures carefully. Then turn the page and see if you can remember what the signs mean.

TURN LEFT
(PUT SIGNS THE OPPOSITE WAY TO SHOW RIGHT TURN)

BROKEN TWIG

BIG STONE WITH A SMALL ONE ON THE LEFT

45°

TWIGS

TILTED STICK

SMALL STONES

MESSAGE HIDDEN

THE NUMBERS SHOW HOW MANY PACES TO GO TO FIND THE MESSAGE

CAUTION

TWIGS

STONES

GONE HOME (END OF TRAIL)

GONE TO HIDEOUT

Trail tips

Remember, a good trail layer only leaves signs where they are really needed. Use them to show a change of direction, or where there is a choice of paths. If there is no path, leave signs about every 20 paces. Try to follow the trail in this picture without turning back to check the signs.

On the trail

Test how well you now know the trail signs. Follow the 'ground signs' here until you come to a 'message hidden' sign. This will give you a clue to where to pick up the trail again. You will only understand it if you have followed the route correctly from the beginning. It starts at a place for learners . . .

GO TO OTHER POND AND READ THE SIGN.

RED LION INN

DOG AND DUCK INN

PICK UP TRAIL AT THE OTHER CHURCH.

PICK UP TRAIL AT THE INN WITH THE TWINKLY NAME.

CHURCH POND

WEST WOOD

SCHOOL

Turn to page 191 to check what you find.

NORTH STAR INN

JOLLY DRUID'S INN

FOX INN

DRUID'S POND

AT POST OFFICE CROSSROADS, GO IN OPPOSITE DIRECTION TO THAT IN TWINKLY NAME.

DRUID'S GROVE

POST OFFICE

CONTINUE TRAIL AT CHURCH NEAR POND- NOT 'OTHER' CHURCH OR 'OTHER' POND.

LONG LAKE

N
W   E
S

101

Indian signs

Use these signs for messages when you are on the trail. Chalk them on stones or scratch them on dry earth. They are based on the picture writing used by Sioux Indians, who scratched messages on dried animal skins and pieces of tree bark.

Time of day

MORNING NOON EVENING DAY NIGHT

Weather and landscape

GRASS ROAD RAIN SUN

LAKE RIVER SEA TREE FOREST

Camp

HIDEOUT (CAMP) CAMPFIRE RATIONS MEETING

HIDDEN OR HIDE LEADER DISCOVERY MANY (HEAP)

Indian messages

These messages were left for you by your Contact. Can you work out what they mean? Use your imagination and a bit of guesswork. Don't 'read' the signs one by one, like words in a sentence. You can check your answers on page 191.

Secret ground signs

You can use these secret ground signs to pass messages to your Contacts which only you and they will understand. First you must all agree what each of the signs means, and where each of you will leave your messages. You can also use them when you are laying a trail.

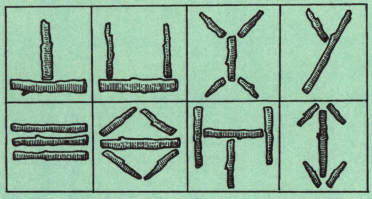

Make signs like these with bits of stick to tell your Contact where to collect messages. They could say 'Behind the gate' or 'Under the mat'.

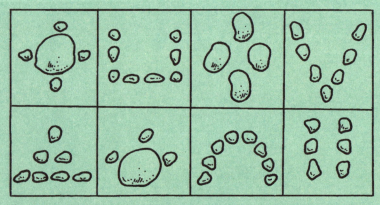

Here are some signs made with stones. Use them to leave warning messages such as 'Avoid the Hideout' or 'You are being followed'.

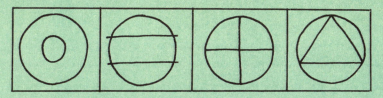

Make these signs with a piece of chalk on a flat stone to tell your Contact who the Opposition spies are.

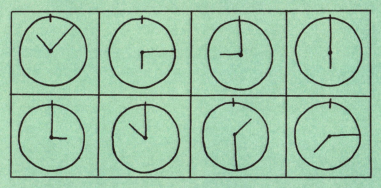

Use signs like these to tell your Contact when to meet you. Draw a circle on a post, wall or flat stone, and add a small mark to show 12 o'clock. Then put in the hands to show the time.

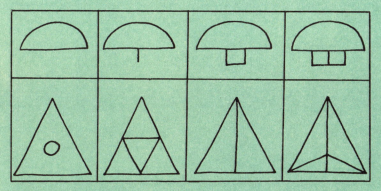

Use these signs to tell your Contact where he or she can meet you. By using two signs together you could leave a message such as, 'Meet me behind the church at six'.

Man-made tracks

To be a good tracker, you should study footprints and car or bicycle tracks when you are on a trail. If they have been made by your Quarry, they may give you useful clues — such as how fast he or she is moving and which way they are heading. They may also show whether the Quarry has stopped or met anyone else.

Tracks show up best in soft ground. Try looking for them in loose earth, mud, snow or in firm sand. You should look for clearly marked, fresh footprints and other marks. If you find dry, cracked tracks, or if there are puddles in footprints, the tracks are old and were probably not made by your Quarry.

Remember to look out for obvious clues. Does your Quarry have a dog with them, or are they using a walking stick? They might be carrying something heavy, or be limping, which would slow them down. Check the size of any footprints you find to see if they could have been made by your Quarry. Look at the next page for some more clues.

The front wheel of a bicycle makes a loopy track as the cyclist turns it from side to side to keep his balance.

As he goes faster he turns it less, so the loops are flatter. The narrow end of the loops point in the direction where the cyclist is heading.

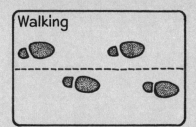

Walking

If your Quarry is walking slowly, you will see whole footprints. Both toe and heel will show.

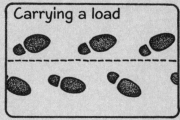

Carrying a load

If your Quarry is carrying a heavy load, the footprints will be deeper and spread farther apart.

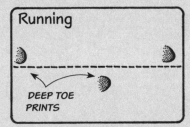

Running

DEEP TOE PRINTS

The prints of a running Quarry will be in a line. If they are going fast, only toe prints will show.

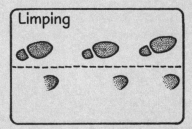

Limping

If they are limping, one footprint will be deep, and you will only be able to see part of the other.

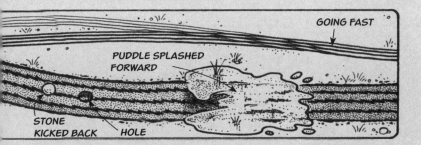

GOING FAST

PUDDLE SPLASHED FORWARD

STONE KICKED BACK   HOLE

You can tell which of two tracks is more recent because the newer track will cut across the older one. The stone kicked back and the puddle splashed forward show the direction that the car which left the tracks was driving in.

Track puzzle

The tracks in the snow tell a whole story. This is Station Road, half an hour after the accident which later made headline news in the local newspaper. Can you work out what happened? Check your answers on page 191.

Tracking signs

There are lots of signs you can look out for when you are on a trail. The clues will vary according to the sort of ground you are walking on and if it is wet or dry. If you are a good tracker you will notice these things so you can look for signs in the right places.

When you are trailing a Quarry, look around you very carefully. A small sign might be a big clue. It is a good idea to try observing things whenever you are out in the country or a park. Try stopping every now and again to listen for noises. Remember that animals and birds can show that someone is moving around.

In woodlands, look at the ground. If someone has walked through dead leaves recently they may have made a trail. The leaves that have been turned over will be damp and darker than top ones.

Look for trails in long grass. If someone has walked through it, you will be able to see where the stems have been pushed apart. If they sat down, the grass will be flat and the stems crushed.

Look for trails, like this, in soft sand. There will be small hollows where someone has walked instead of footprints.

Look at the grass under any object you find. If it is pale or yellow, it means the object has been there for quite a few days.

On dry, dusty ground look for small stones which have been kicked around. There may be scuff marks from a Quarry's shoes.

Twigs are sometimes bent or broken by someone walking on them. If a break is new, the wood will be bright and pale.

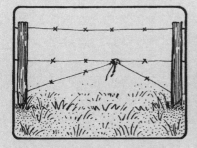

Someone crawling under a fence has hooked up the wire. There is a thread of torn clothes and the grass is flattened underneath.

Animals such as sheep, running as if frightened, may mean someone is there, possibly creeping along the other side of the hedge.

Picking up a trail

When you are following a trail you may lose your Quarry, particularly in woods or where a path divides. If you do, try to find the trail again quickly. Look around you for obvious signs, such as birds suddenly flying up or animals running away.

Listen hard for noises which might give you a clue, such as the rustle of someone walking through dry leaves. Your Quarry may sing or whistle, not knowing he or she is being followed.

Next look carefully at the ground. If you find a
fresh footprint, note which way it is pointing and go
in that direction. If you don't find footprints, try
walking around your starting point, searching hard.
Walk in an increasing circle until you find a clue.

The picture below shows the trail left by a Quarry
who is now out of sight. See if you can spot the
clues which show which path he or she has taken.
Check your answers on page 191.

Hoof prints

Whenever you are out in the country or in any open ground, try out your stalking and tracking skills. This will help you to notice small signs when you are on the trail of a Quarry who is out of sight.

Look carefully at patches of wet earth, wet sand or snow where prints show up well. You can also see them on grass or leaves after rain.

Horses and cows

The hoofs of horses, wild ponies and cows are about the same size but have different shapes.

If a horse is shod, you will see only the track of its shoes (a). If it is unshod, you will see an almost round track with a dent at the back (b).

If a horse is going fast, you may see scuff marks in front of each hoof mark. Cows have split hoofs (c).

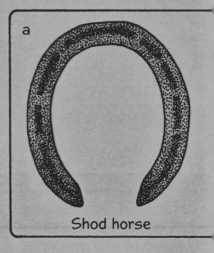

a

Shod horse

Deer, sheep and goats

Deer, sheep and goats also have split hoofs, like cows, but they are much smaller. When you find small hoof prints like these, look for other clues. If they have been made by sheep, look for bits of wool caught on hedges or wire fences. Deer sometimes nibble the bark off trees just up from the ground.

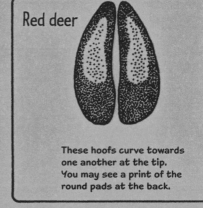

Red deer

These hoofs curve towards one another at the tip. You may see a print of the round pads at the back.

Learn to recognize animal prints and to see which way the animals went. Try stalking very quietly to see how close you can get to an animal before it is frightened away. This is also a good test of your camouflage clothes. Remember that some animals can be dangerous if you go too near. Keep away from any animals that have young babies with them.

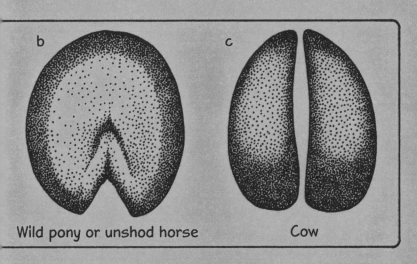

b **c**

Wild pony or unshod horse   Cow

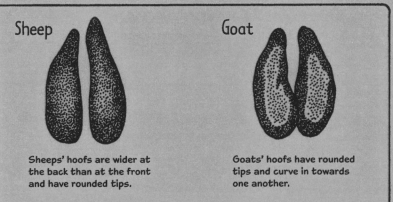

Sheep   Goat

Sheeps' hoofs are wider at the back than at the front and have rounded tips.

Goats' hoofs have rounded tips and curve in towards one another.

Paw prints

To be a good tracker, you need to learn to recognize all the footprints you see. It is useful to know if your Quarry is accompanied by a dog, and if it is a big dog. You may have to change your tracking methods if it is. Remember that dogs have a very keen sense of smell and may know you are there, even if it and your Quarry cannot see you.

Dogs sometimes run out and bark at strangers or follow them for a while. If this happened as your Quarry tried to sneak past a house, the dog tracks might give them away—although your Quarry was careful not to leave any tracks themselves.

The prints made by dogs and cats often look alike but a dog's prints are usually larger. It is useful if you learn to tell them apart. Look at the prints on the next page to see how they are different. It is a good idea to watch a dog or cat crossing some mud or sand. Then look at the trail it has made. Examine the tracks carefully and see how they change when the cat or dog walks slowly and then runs.

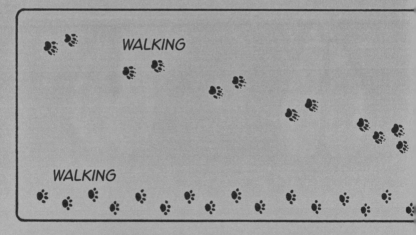

WALKING

WALKING

Dog print

Dog prints usually look like this, although they may be bigger or smaller. The pad is shaped like a triangle and there are four toe prints. The pad mark is larger than the toes. There is one longish claw mark at the end of each toe. The claws may be worn down.

Cat print

You can tell the difference between dog and cat tracks because cat tracks are small and do not have claw marks. The claw marks show only if the cat has landed on the ground after jumping from a height. When cats walk, they draw their claws into the ends of their toes.

RUNNING

LEAPING

Bird tracks

If you live in a town where you are not likely to see the footprints of horses and wild animals, look for bird prints instead. This is good tracking experience and you can pick up quite a lot of clues about birds. Look for bird prints in gardens, parks, on the edges of lakes and ponds, in zoos and wildlife parks. Birds which live mostly in bushes and trees are usually small and light. They have pointed claws and a long back toe to grip branches. They often hop along the ground, looking for food.

Larger, heavier birds, such as partridges and pheasants, have short, strong feet for running along the ground. Their tracks run almost in a straight line or in a zigzag. Look for wading bird tracks in sand or mud on the banks of rivers or ponds. You might see the webbed feet of swimming birds too.

The opposite page has instructions on how to make a Track Trap. Birds walking across it will leave clear footprints.

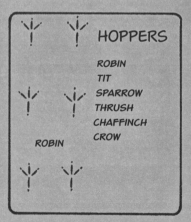

HOPPERS

ROBIN
TIT
SPARROW
THRUSH
CHAFFINCH
CROW

ROBIN

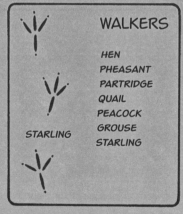

WALKERS

HEN
PHEASANT
PARTRIDGE
QUAIL
PEACOCK
GROUSE
STARLING

STARLING

TRACK TRAP

ON A DRY DAY, LAY THE BROWN PAPER ON THE GROUND AND SPREAD FLOUR AROUND THE EDGES.

YOU WILL NEED :

SHEET OF BROWN PAPER
SOME FLOUR
BREAD CRUMBS

BROWN PAPER

THIN
LAYER
OF
FLOUR

WITH A BIT OF LUCK YOU SHOULD FIND SOME TRACKS ON THE PAPER NEXT MORNING.

PUT SOME BREADCRUMBS IN THE MIDDLE OF THE SHEET. LEAVE THEM OVERNIGHT.

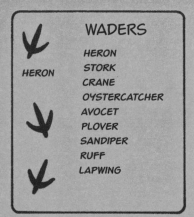

WADERS

HERON

HERON
STORK
CRANE
OYSTERCATCHER
AVOCET
PLOVER
SANDIPER
RUFF
LAPWING

SWIMMERS

SWAN

SWAN
DUCK
GOOSE
GULL
CORMORANT
GUILLEMOT
GREBE
TERN

Making plaster casts

A collection of plaster casts is very useful for tracking experience. Casts which are a copy of the foot or paw which made the track are called negative. Casts which copy the track itself are called positive. Use negative casts to make trails for tracking practice, and positive ones to help you recognize tracks.

Try to make casts from clear, complete tracks. The ground should be firm and level. Note the animal or bird, the date and place. Scratch this on the cast later.

You will need:

1. A bag of plaster of Paris
2. Strips of cardboard about 18cm (6in) long and 6cm (2in) wide
3. Paper clips
4. A jar half full of water
5. Teaspoon and old toothbrush
6. Vaseline or grease
7. Newspaper for wrapping the finished casts
8. Pieces of string

Grease the inside of a cardboard strip, so that the plaster will not stick. Fix it around the track, using a paper clip.

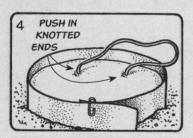

Push a bit of string deep down into one side of the cast before it hardens. You will be able to hang it up by this later on.

When the cast has set (after about 20 minutes), pull off the cardboard. You can rub off any loose soil with an old toothbrush.

Using plaster of Paris

You can buy plaster of Paris in hardware stores. Here are some tips:

1 Pour the plaster into the water, stirring with your free hand. A pinch of salt makes it dry faster. Don't add the water to the plaster, as it will go lumpy.

2 Touch it to see if it has set. At first it will be warm, but it will dry as it cools.

3 Plaster sets quickly. Never pour it down a drain, or it will block it up. Pour left-over plaster on newspaper, then throw it out. Rinse the spoon and jar immediately.

Slowly pour plaster into a small jar of water, stirring all the time, until it is smooth and runny like thick cream.

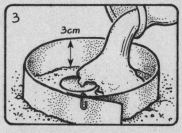

Before the mixture dries, pour it steadily over the track. Pour from one side until the cast is about 3cm (1in) thick.

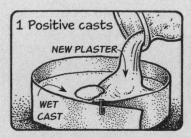

Turn the negative cast over inside the cardboard and smear the top with soapy water. Now pour on the next layer of wet plaster.

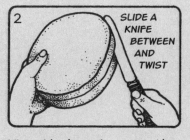

When this plaster has set and is hard, pull off the cardboard wall. Gently separate the two casts with a knife, like this.

Useful measurements

To be a Good Spy, you can use your own body measurements to work out the size of footprints, distances and the height of your Quarry.

Take your own measurements with a ruler or tape measure. Remember them or write them on this chart. You will have to change them every six months if you are still growing.

By knowing the length of your own shoes, you can guess how tall your Quarry is by the size of his or her footprints. Short people usually have small feet. Tall people have big feet. Measure the length of your stride and use it to guess how tall your Quarry is. Tall people usually walk with big strides. Short people and women usually take shorter steps.

You can also use the length of your stride to work out distances. Count your steps as you walk along. Then multiply the number of steps by the size of your stride to get the distance. Use the other measurements to work out the heights of people and things.

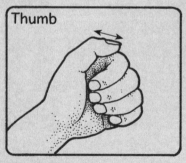

Thumb

Hold your thumb like this to measure from the tip to the joint accurately.

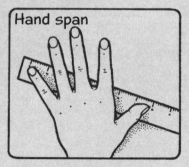

Hand span

Spread your hand out as wide as you can, like this. Lay it across a flat ruler.

Reach Height

Stand up straight with your back against a wall and your heels together to measure your height.

Stride

Take an ordinary stride and measure the distance from the toe of one shoe to the toe of the other.

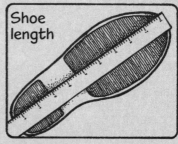

Shoe length

Measure the exact length of one of your feet from heel to toe.

Arm span

Where 1m (1 yard) comes to

First measure your outstretched arms all the way from one fingertip to the other.

Then cut a piece of string 1m (1 yard) long and see how far across your body it reaches.

Looking at footprints

The best time for looking at footprints is when there is snow on the ground. Otherwise look in wet earth, damp sand or patches of mud. To get clues from footprints about the person who made them, rehearse at home with different kinds and sizes of shoes and boots.

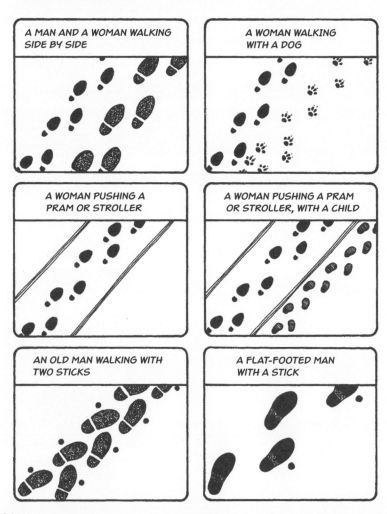

A MAN AND A WOMAN WALKING SIDE BY SIDE

A WOMAN WALKING WITH A DOG

A WOMAN PUSHING A PRAM OR STROLLER

A WOMAN PUSHING A PRAM OR STROLLER, WITH A CHILD

AN OLD MAN WALKING WITH TWO STICKS

A FLAT-FOOTED MAN WITH A STICK

Here are various different kinds of boots and shoes. Can you match them up with the footprints in the second box?

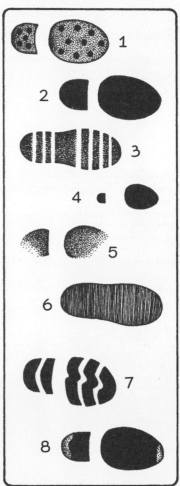

Answers

A = 2, B = 6, C = 8, D = 4, E = 7, F = 3, G = 5, H = 1

Spy spotter's sketchbook

If you want to be a Good Spy, you'll find it useful to
be able to draw people's faces. Then you can keep
a record of what Enemy Spies look like. The parts
of a face, such as eyes, nose and ears, are called
features. The next four pages show you how to draw
people's faces and where the features go.

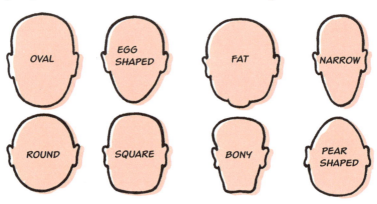

Head shapes

Everybody's head is a different shape. Use these head shapes to copy or
trace. Choose the shape that you think is most like the head of the
person you want to draw.

Where features go

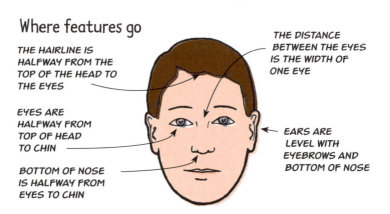

THE HAIRLINE IS
HALFWAY FROM THE
TOP OF THE HEAD TO
THE EYES

THE DISTANCE
BETWEEN THE EYES
IS THE WIDTH OF
ONE EYE

EYES ARE
HALFWAY FROM
TOP OF HEAD
TO CHIN

EARS ARE
LEVEL WITH
EYEBROWS AND
BOTTOM OF NOSE

BOTTOM OF NOSE
IS HALFWAY FROM
EYES TO CHIN

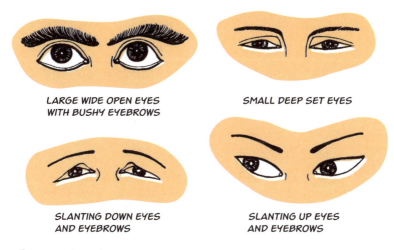

LARGE WIDE OPEN EYES
WITH BUSHY EYEBROWS

SMALL DEEP SET EYES

SLANTING DOWN EYES
AND EYEBROWS

SLANTING UP EYES
AND EYEBROWS

Eyes and eyebrows

Here are four different pairs of eyes. Eyes are difficult to draw because
you need to get really close to people to see their shape and shade.

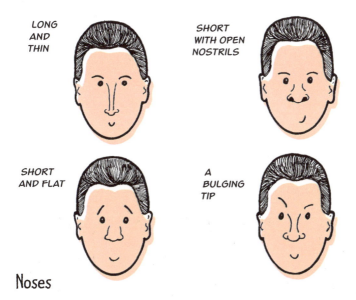

LONG
AND
THIN

SHORT
WITH OPEN
NOSTRILS

SHORT
AND FLAT

A
BULGING
TIP

Noses

These pictures show what different shaped noses look like from the front.
On the next page you can see how to draw them from the side as well.

More for your sketchbook

The side of a face is called a profile, and it is much more difficult to disguise than the front of a face.

Noses

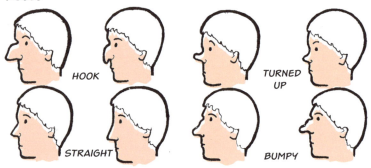

Noses are difficult to disguise in profile. They stick out and they come in many different shapes and sizes.

Ears

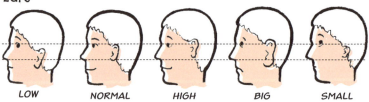

The tops of most people's ears are on a level with their eyes. Ears are usually twice as long as they are wide. They come in many different shapes and sizes.

Chins

These pictures show what a man would look like with different chins. No disguise would hide a big chin, except a real or false beard.

Hair

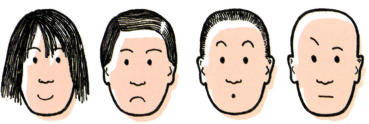

These pictures show how the same man can make himself look different, if he changes the style and length of his hair or wears a wig.

Beards

Beards and moustaches are some of the most common disguises. So it is important to learn to draw them and notice how they change a face.

Hats and glasses

Here is the same man again looking quite different in each picture. Would you guess he was the same man as the one in the top row?

Why disguise?

Good Spies wear disguises so that they won't be recognized by the Enemy Spies. Then they can watch them without being discovered, and keep them guessing by changing their disguises.

Try to avoid being photographed. Then the Enemy Spies will not have a record of your face.

Choose your disguise carefully. Try to wear clothes which help you fit into your surroundings.

When you are out on a spying mission at night or during the day, always try to act in a way that looks ordinary.

Whenever you can, use cover such as trees to keep watch on suspicious-looking people without them knowing.

Change your disguises as often as you can. Then the watching Enemy will not know who is the spy.

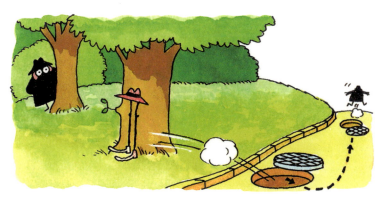

Use different tricks to get away from the Enemy. Keep them waiting and watching long after you have gone.

Quick cover-ups

Your secret spying missions will only be successful if the Enemy Spies do not recognize you. Here are a few tricks to help keep your face hidden from them. Always be prepared to take action. You never know where the next Enemy Spy may be.

1 Newspaper trick

You are out keeping watch on a building when an Enemy Spy comes around the corner.

You carefully raise your newspaper, peering over the top as the spy comes towards you. Then, out of the corner of your eye, you spot a second spy, a short distance behind the first one.

Now you must keep an eye on them both, making sure neither of them can see your face.

When both have passed, you can fold up your paper and follow them to their secret destination.

Always carry a handkerchief in your pocket. Whip it out and use it in an emergency.

An umbrella is another useful piece of equipment for hiding your face in moments of danger.

Pretend to drop some money. But make sure that an Enemy Spy does not try to join in.

If you are carrying a bag or case, bend all the way over and pretend to look for something in it.

In a real emergency, the only way to keep your face hidden might be to bend down suddenly and pretend to tie your shoelace.

Decoys

Enemy Spies will feel really safe only if they are quite sure they know where you are. Here are some cunning ways to keep them waiting while you go to your next assignment.

Spies often do their most secret work at night. Never leave your bed unoccupied even when you are away on a night mission. Leave a dummy under the sheets to trick the Enemy Spy.

This trick shows how to collect a secret document from HQ, and escape without being followed.

The spy outside watches you go in. The light goes on and he sees your shadow at the window.

1 Who's watching who?

Who is the mysterious person behind the fence who just goes on watching hour after hour?

2

Nobody feels safe if they are being watched. Imagine how this spy feels trapped upstairs.

3

But it is your dummy that sits in front of the window, while you prepare to escape.

4

The Enemy Spy soon gets tired of watching you in your HQ. Now you can slip away into the night.

Hints and warnings

Here are some ideas that will help you to be a better spy and move about unrecognized when you are on a secret mission. It is important to wear clothes that help you to fit in with your surroundings.

Bright lights

Always keep in the shadows at night. Avoid the glare of street lights and lighted windows.

Familiar smells

Beware of dogs that know you. They will recognize you even though you are well disguised.

Bluff

You can help a friend to spy by causing a diversion. This attracts the Enemy Spy's attention.

1 Double bluff

Try this trick. Two of you dress exactly the same. Hide your faces as you pass an Enemy Spy.

1 Fitting in

If you are spying on a building that is guarded, it is important to think of a good disguise or you will be quickly spotted.

One good way to baffle an Enemy Spy is to wear the same sort of clothes as local people so that you blend in.

When you have passed by, he will be sure to follow, hoping you will lead him back to your HQ.

Now you separate and both set off in different directions. He won't know which one to follow.

139

Detecting disguises

However good your own disguise is, it is just as important to be able to recognize when other people are in disguise. You will only be prepared for the sort of tricks the Enemy Spies will try to play on you if you are quite sure they really are spies.

Here are a few ways of checking up on suspicious people. Try them out on your friends at home first, then you will know exactly what to do when you meet a suspect.

See how this Good Spy tests if the lady suspect is a spy too. He rushes up to give her a big hug.

She is so surprised that he is able to feel for any padding or secret pockets in her clothes.

1 Shockers

If you suspect that a woman is really a man in disguise, give her a shock and listen to the scream.

2

When she turns and runs away, you will easily be able to see if it really is a woman, or a man.

1 Wet hand shake

2

Carry a damp sponge in your raincoat pocket. If a person looks as if they are wearing hand make-up, quickly rub your fingers on the sponge and shake their hand firmly. Some of the make-up may come off.

False beard trick

To get a close look at a suspicious-looking beard, pretend you can see an insect caught in it.

Clean up

If you think someone might be disguised, offer to rub a smudge off their face with your handkerchief.

Watching people

Before choosing a disguise, it is a good idea to spend time watching other people to see how they behave. But remember, most people don't like being stared at and some of them might be spies too.

Look at people when they are asleep. Some open their mouths and snore. Others let their heads fall forwards.

People do funny things with their legs when they are sitting down. Some cross them over, others waggle their feet.

Habits

Only very well trained spies are able to change their habits when in disguise. If you watch people waiting at a bus stop, you will see how many different ways there are of just standing and waiting. People's habits become even more obvious when they start moving and doing things. Build up a file of how people behave and try copying them.

WAITING	WALKING

Watch how people carry things. See if they are used to doing it.

People have different ways of eating. Some eat slowly and carefully. Others eat very fast and spill things.

Try looking at people from behind. Back views are difficult to disguise. Which of the two people here might be the man?

RUNNING	STALKING	YAWNING	TALKING

Secret mission

Undercover Agent 9412X (code name Zed) is ordered by Headquarters to collect a file of secret plans. It has been put in a left luggage locker at the international airport. Zed has been sent the key and warned that the Enemy Spies have been tipped off. They know the file is hidden somewhere in the airport and are watching, hoping to grab it. Can Zed get the file safely away without being spotted?

ZED GOES TO THE AIRPORT IN A TAXI . . .

. . . DISGUISED AS A PASSENGER FLYING TO A FOREIGN CITY.

HE GOES INTO A ROOM, UNOBSERVED.

QUICKLY, HE CHANGES INTO A NEW DISGUISE . . .

. . . AS A REPAIR MAN WORKING IN THE AIRPORT.

PRETENDING TO REPAIR THE LOCKERS, HE GETS THE FILE.

LATER, HE PUTS ON ANOTHER DISGUISE . . .

. . . AND PREPARES TO LEAVE.

SAFELY THROUGH THE DOOR, HE HAILS A TAXI.

THE OPPOSITION IS PUZZLED, BUT ZED HAS GOT AWAY.

Spot the mistakes

The Embassy has invited many special guests to a reception, including ambassadors from foreign countries. HQ is tipped off that some Enemy Spies disguised as guests and waiters may try to attend to gather secret information. How many suspicious-looking people can you see? There are at least 20.

Spy challenge

This is a spy game for two players. The boxes below show you how to make the board and stand-up spies.

You will need:

1. White cardboard, about 24x24cm (9x9in)
2. Thin cardboard for the spy stand-ups
3. A ruler and a pencil
4. Paint and glue
5. A paint brush

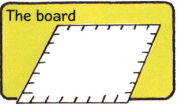

The board

Draw seven marks 3cm (1in) apart along each side of the board. Rule lines from the top to bottom marks and from the sides.

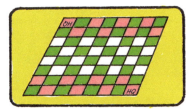

Paint the squares like this. The red squares are the spies' home territory. Write HQ on the red squares in two corners.

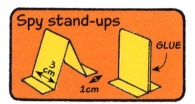

Spy stand-ups

GLUE

Cut out 16 strips of thin cardboard, each 7x3cm (3x1in). Fold them in half and bend out the ends. Glue the two halves.

Paint spy faces on one side. On the other side, for each player, draw an M on one stand-up and numbers 1 to 7 on the others.

The game

Each player has seven spies, worth 1 to 7 points, and a Master Spy, worth 8 points. The idea is for each player to move his spies from their home territory into enemy home territory. The Master Spy must reach enemy HQ. On the way, spies can challenge and capture enemy spies.

How to play

Each player puts his spies on the red squares at his end of the board. Players move a spy one square each turn. Spies may only move diagonally, but they can move either backwards or forwards.

Players may not miss a turn, but they don't have to challenge an enemy spy. To challenge, a spy must land on the square next to an enemy spy. The player then says, 'I challenge you'. The spy with the highest number wins and the loser goes off the board. If a spy challenges a Master Spy, the spy goes off the board and the player loses 10 points. If a Master Spy challenges another Master Spy, both stay on the board, but the challenger loses 10 points.

The game ends when one player has all his remaining men in enemy territory, and his Master Spy in the enemy HQ.

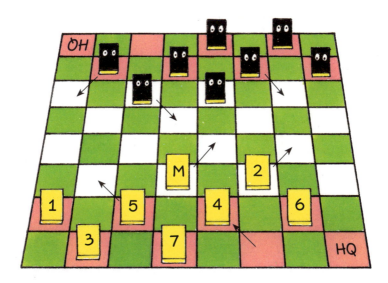

How to score

Add up the numbers on your spies in enemy territory. Take away from your score any points you have lost during the game. The first person with all his remaining spies home and his Master Spy in enemy HQ adds 10 points. The player with the most points wins.

Spot the spies

This game is a test of Good Spy disguises. Two people can play or as many as you like. All the spies arrange to be at one place, on one day, at a certain time. They can choose a main shopping street, a park or anywhere with lots of people. It helps the game if there is a clock at the chosen place.

Each spy then dresses up in a really Good Spy disguise, so that no one will be able to recognize them.

They go to the place at the right time and stay there for a certain time (that's why the clock is useful). They move around, trying to spot the other spies, but without being seen by them. Good Spies always pretend to have a reason to be where they are.

Each spy carries a notebook and a pencil. He writes down the names of each of the spies he spots and each bit of disguise they are wearing, such as a wig, a big black hat, padded stomach, a false moustache or big shoes.

Each spy also makes notes of what the other spies are doing. They might pretend to be shopping or delivering a package in the street. If it is in a park, they might pretend to feed the pigeons or fly a kite.

When the time is up, all the spies go home and take off their disguises. They then meet at the Good Spy Headquarters — anywhere will do.

Each spy scores a point for every right bit of disguise and right bit of pretend action he has written down in his notebook. He loses a point for every wrong bit written down. The spy with the biggest score is the winner. He is then called the Master Spy.

Which hat?

A Good Spy may be sent on a secret mission at any time to anywhere in the world. He must wear the right clothes so he won't be noticed. Here is a Good Spy's hat cupboard.

1

2

Which hat or headdress would he choose for these seven different places in the world? Look at the pictures and then decide on a hat. Check your answers at the bottom of the page.

Answers

1 A Russian fur hat
2 A Scottish tartan cap
3 A Mexican straw hat
4 An American cowboy hat
5 An Arab head cloth
6 A Swiss lady's lace cap
7 An Australian bush hat

153

Quick disguise collection

A Good Spy needs lots of clothes, bags, shoes, boots, hats, gloves, belts, scarves, walking sticks, umbrellas, sunglasses, glasses and cheap accessories. Collect as many different kinds as you can and hide them in your secret disguise cupboard.

Try asking your family and their grown-up friends for old clothes and other things they don't want any more. You may also be able to buy clothes and things very cheaply at old clothes sales or markets.

Get the clothes ready so you can put them on quickly when you need to disguise yourself. Put long clothes on hangers, if you can, so they don't get creased and crumpled. Clothes which are too big are useful because they change your shape and you can wear padding underneath.

Clothes too long

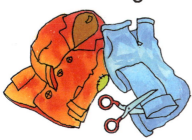

Cut off the ends of sleeves and jeans legs if they are too long. Snip around them neatly.

Cut off the ends of skirts and dresses. Turn the edges in and pin, glue or sew them up.

Stuff paper or bits of cloth into the toes of boots and shoes if they are too big. Or wear your own inside.

Ask a grown-up to take the glass out of old glasses. Rubber bands on the ends will stop them from slipping.

Pin or sew old towels or rolled up material inside large coats — then the padding won't slip out.

Use belts on coats which are too big and to hold up jeans and skirts. They help to change your shape.

Check your equipment

To be a Good Spy when you go on a mission, everything you wear or carry must fit in with your disguise. If you say you are from a certain country, your clothes, luggage, money, family photographs and letters must all come from that country too.

Here are some of the things to make sure you have before you leave your home base.

CUT OUT LABELS WITH MAKER'S NAME

TAKE EVERYTHING OUT OF POCKETS, BRIEFCASE OR HANDBAG

CHECK LABELS IN SHOES

A Good Spy cuts out all the labels from their clothes which might give them away – even shoes, boots and underwear.

Go through your pockets and briefcase. Then put in all the things that back up the person you are pretending to be.

A Good Spy should write themselves letters addressed to the country they say they come from, with the right stamps on them.

Take a handkerchief with the initials of your false name in the corner. And a ballpoint pen with your false initials on it.

DIARY WITH FALSE NAMES AND PLACES

MONEY FROM HOME COUNTRY

NEWSPAPER CUTTING

NOVEMBER
30 Wallpaper at home

DECEMBER
1 Peter's birthday
2 Visit to

FAMILY PHOTOGRAPH

RED SPY SEEN IN TEA ROOM by

RAIL TICKET

BUS TICKET

STAMPS

Get your wallet ready very carefully. Collect things from the country you say you come from. And write up a diary, filling it in with the names of places you say you have visited. This will be very useful if you are challenged and your story is questioned.

How to put on make-up

To be a Good Spy, you need to learn how to use simple make-up to change your looks. You can change your eyes, eyebrows and mouth with the make-up grown-up women use. By putting on shadows and lines, you can make your eyes seem bright or dull and your cheeks full, or hollow and old. You can also make yourself look ill or healthy.

Try putting on make-up in secret in front of a mirror. You need lots of light so that you can see what you are doing. Use a little make-up to start with. It will show up much more in bright daylight than in electric light.

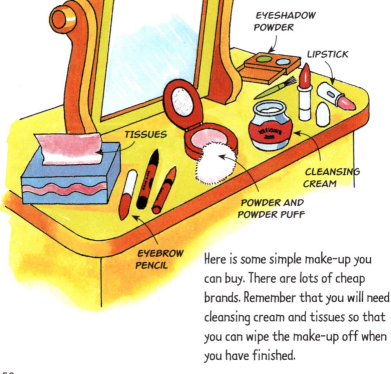

EYESHADOW POWDER

LIPSTICK

TISSUES

CLEANSING CREAM

POWDER AND POWDER PUFF

EYEBROW PENCIL

Here is some simple make-up you can buy. There are lots of cheap brands. Remember that you will need cleansing cream and tissues so that you can wipe the make-up off when you have finished.

Eyebrows

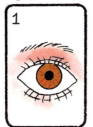 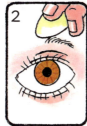  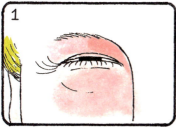

Use this easy trick to alter your eyebrows (1). First rub on thick concealer to blot them out (2).

When your eyebrows have disappeared (3), draw on new eyebrows with a pencil (4).

Eyes

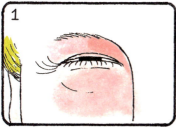 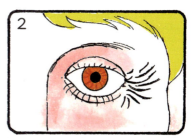

Wrinkle your eyes so you can see the wrinkles at each side of them. See how your eyelids crease.

Draw thin, dark lines with a soft eyebrow pencil along each crease. This makes you look older.

Baggy eyes

The skin under some people's eyes hangs down in bags. Draw them with an eyebrow pencil.

Black eye

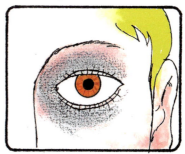

To pretend you have a black eye, brush black and blue eye shadow round your eye. Smudge it a bit.

More make-up tips

Here are some ways of making your face look older. Try using face powder to make it paler. Use dark eye shadow for the shadows. Don't forget to change your hair when you disguise yourself as an old person.

People's faces change as they grow older. Look at old people and you will see that their faces are often thin and pale. They have lines around their eyes and mouths, and their lips are thinner. They often have hollow cheeks.

Rub pale foundation cream over your lips until they are the same shade as the rest of your face.

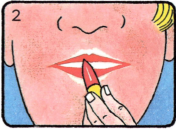

Draw on a new, thin mouth with a very dark red lipstick. Make your lips look small and thin.

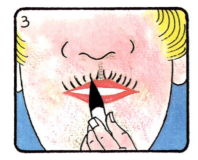

Old people often have wrinkled mouths. Draw thin lines around your mouth with a dark pencil.

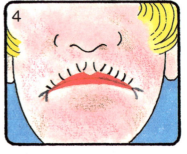

Now make a face, pulling your mouth down at the corners. Draw dark lines where you see creases.

1 Shadows

Look at your face to see where the hollows are. Feel it with your fingers to find the main bones.

2

Try brushing dark shades of eye shadow around your eyes. Shade it at the sides of your face.

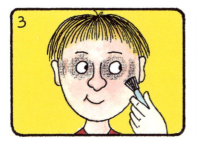

3

Put dark powder shadows where there are hollows between the tops of your ears and your eyes.

4

Brush shadows on your cheeks below your cheek bones. This will make them look hollow.

5

Shadows each side of your nose make it look thin. Dab a dark shade under your nose and mouth.

6

Use a cotton ball to dab pale face powder over the parts of your face where there are no shadows.

Special effects

Enemy Spies will find it much more difficult to recognize you when you wear the sort of special effects shown on these pages. Don't use them too often or the Enemy Spies will soon get to know them.

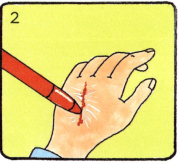

Smear some rubbery glue on to your skin. As it dries, pinch the skin together to make it look like a cut.

Use red paint or felt tip along the lines of the cut. Then make dark stitch marks along each side.

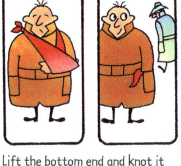

You need a friend to help you make a sling like this. Fold a scarf or piece of cloth (1). Hold your arm across it, and put one end around your neck (2).

Lift the bottom end and knot it to the one around your neck (3). Once the sling is made, you can slip it on and off quickly to fool the Enemy Spies.

Black teeth

Pretend you have lost some of your front teeth. Cut out small squares of gummed black paper and stick them on your teeth.

Eye patch

Cut out a piece of cardboard shaped like this. Paint it black on one side. Make holes at the top corners and tie on black elastic.

1 Bandage

Use a roll of bandage, or a long strip of ordinary white material. Begin with it rolled up.

2

Bind it as tightly as you can so it won't slip. Fix the end with a safety pin, or tuck it in.

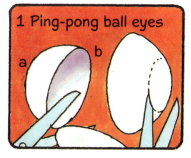

1 Ping-pong ball eyes

Carefully cut a ping-pong ball in half with scissors (a). Then cut a small, round hole in each half (b).

2

Shade the ping-pong ball halves blue. Make small holes in each. Join with elastic to hold them on.

Change your walk

A Good Spy changes his walk to fit the disguise he is wearing. He knows he can easily be recognized in a crowd by the way he walks. Even if he is well disguised and the Enemy Spies are too far away to see his face clearly, they may guess who he is.

Everyone moves their arms and holds their hands in different ways. This, too, can give away a good disguise, if it doesn't fit with a certain way of walking. Here are some walks to rehearse.

Stiff leg

Try walking with one stiff leg. Tie a scarf around one knee to make it difficult to bend.

Limp

Limp on one leg, walking as if it hurts. Put something in one shoe to remind you which leg it is.

Strutting

Walk quickly with your head up. Lean back and hold your hands behind you. Take big strides.

Slouching

Take small steps and shuffle your feet. Put your hands in your pockets and hunch your shoulders.

High-heeled totter

Wear high-heeled shoes and take very small steps. Bend your knees and bounce as you walk.

Low-heeled shuffle

Wear large flat shoes and shuffle along, taking very small steps. Lean forward with your head down.

Toes in

Turn your toes in as you walk. This makes you move in quite a different way. Lean forward a little.

Toes out

Turn your toes out as far as you can and bend your knees. Put your feet down flat and stomp a bit.

Striding

Walk quickly with big strides, and swing your arms. Put your heels down first as you stride.

Bent back

Bend sideways and put your hand on that hip as if you have a bad back. Walk slowly.

Looking fat

One of the best ways to disguise yourself is to change your shape. If you are thin, make yourself look like a fat person. Here are some hints on how to do it. Watch how fat people move and behave. This will give you lots of ideas for disguises, and hints on how to act as a fat, heavy person.

You can make your stomach look big by tying one or two cushions around your waist. Wrap a small towel around your shoulders to make them look broad. Tie scarves around your legs and arms to fill out your jeans and sleeves. Wear big clothes over your normal ones. Put on big shoes and gloves.

Fat people often look redder in the face than other people. Rub some lipstick on your cheeks to make them red. Wear a high collar so your neck doesn't give you away.

A fat person gets out of breath easily. When pretending to be a fat person, puff and pant from time to time. Mop your forehead as if you are too hot.

A fat person will quite often lean slightly backwards to balance himself as he walks along. He may also stand with his feet wide apart for better balance.

Fat people usually move slowly and have some difficulty getting up and sitting down. They use their hands a lot to lower and raise themselves, especially in big chairs.

Looking old

Disguising yourself as an old person is great fun. Remember that people change a lot as they grow older. Here are some things to think about when preparing your disguise.

Make yourself look like an old person by wearing clothes that are too big and are dull shades. They should also look bulky and warm. Dark hats and scarves and glasses help with this sort of disguise.

An old person disguise is often useful on a secret mission. Knitting can be a good excuse for sitting and watching.

Old people are often a bit unsteady, so move slowly. Remember to hold on to things such as banisters when coming down stairs.

Most old people look friendly and innocent.
A spy disguised as an old person should
not be spotted by the Enemy.

Pretending to shop or look in shop windows is a good way of hiding in a
group of people. The disguise is also a good reason to walk slowly and
stop often for a rest. This is useful when collecting information.

Old people often stoop a little.
This makes them seem shorter.
They shuffle their feet along and
use walking sticks.

Pretend to be very stiff. Bending
down slowly to pick something up
off the ground is a good way to
have a look around.

169

Secret hiding places

A Good Spy often has to carry secret messages, films or documents from one place to another, or to give to their Contact. Some of these may be small, but you will need hiding places in your clothes in case you are stopped and searched by Enemy Spies.

You can make secret pockets in your spy clothes. There are lots of other places to hide small things in, so they are easy to get at when you want them.

1 Secret pocket

Carefully cut a few stitches along the bottom of the lining of an old coat. Undo one side only.

2

Pull up the lining. Stitch a pocket, cut from an old coat, into the coat. Pull down the lining again.

1 Secret slots

Cut a piece of thin cardboard about 10cm (4in) long and just thinner than a wide belt.

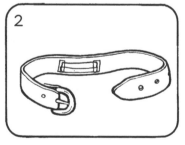

2

Stick the ends and bottom of the cardboard to the inside of the belt. Use sticky tape or glue.

Wigs, hats, caps and berets

Put secret messages or letters on top of your head before you put on a wig. Fold them up first. Bulky papers can go under a big hat. Hide smaller things under a cap or in a beret.

Hat bands

If you have to take your hat off, hide small messages behind the inside or outside band.

Collars

Tuck small messages under your collar, or push them up under the roll collar of a sweater.

Cuffs

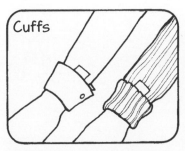

Messages can go inside folded cuffs of shirts or sweaters. They are easy to slip in and out.

Turn-ups

If you have turn-ups on your disguise jeans, roll up papers. Curve them to fit inside.

More secret hiding places

1 Shoes

If you look inside most shoes you will find a thin inner sole. Pull up this sole from some old shoes.

2

Slide a secret message under the sole. Press it down. It won't show when the shoes are off.

Socks and boots

Fold secret messages or papers into long thin strips. Slide them down your socks or long boots.

Tie

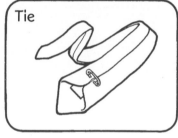

Look at the back of a tie. It has a fold all the way down. Slide a message in and pin it to the back.

Badge

Fold a secret paper very small. Stick it to the back of a badge or brooch with tape. Then pin it on.

Scarf

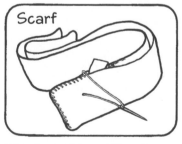

Fold a long, wide scarf lengthways. Sew up one end and part of one side. Slip in your secret message.

Newspaper

Slip large papers in a folded newspaper, magazine or comic. Carry it under your arm.

Record sleeve

Slide large thin papers into a record sleeve. Push them well down. Carry the record sleeve openly.

1 Umbrella

Open an umbrella. Roll documents around the handle. A rubber band will keep them in place.   Close

2

the umbrella loosely to hide the documents. Remember them if it rains.

Guitar case

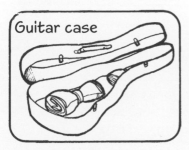

Carry very large bundles of secret papers in a guitar case. Or any musical instrument case will do.

Shopping bag

Hide secret papers in the bottom of a shopping bag. Cover them with fruit or vegetables.

False noses

To make a false nose, use pale pink or pale brown model clay. Knead it like this to make it soft.

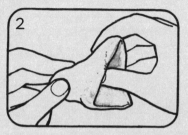

Press the clay into a nose shape. Don't make it too big or it will be heavy and may fall off.

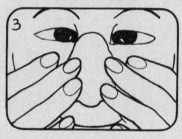

Press the nose over your own. Leave it open at the end so you can breathe. Smooth the edges.

Shape the nose again. Hold up a second mirror so you see what you look like from the side too.

Rub make-up over your face and the new nose. Then they will both look the same shade.

If you think the nose might fall off, put on glasses. They will rest on it and hold it in place.

Hands and nails

1 Hands

To make your hands look old, put blue shadows on your fingers. Rub it between the joints.

2

You will see pale blue lines on the back of your hand. Draw on them with a blue pencil like this.

3

Now clench your fist. Rub blue pencil between your knuckles to make them look hollow.

4

Rub pale powder into your skin. This will make it look old and wrinkly. Dust it around your nails.

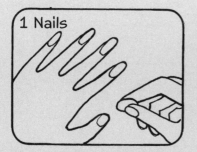

1 Nails

Cut ten nail shapes out of thin white cardboard. Stick them on your nails with quick-drying glue.

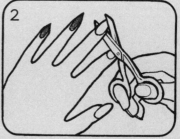

2

Trim the nails evenly. Paint them pink or red with water paint. Or try making different shapes.

Moustaches

Try making lots of different kinds and shapes of moustaches to see which one suits you best. All false facial hair should match your own hair.

The quickest way to give yourself a moustache is to draw or paint one straight on to your skin. Use a brown or black wax crayon or eyebrow pencil to do this.

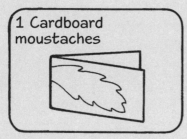

Fold a piece of cardboard in half and draw this outline on the side of it. Cut it out and paint it.

Wrap sticky tape around your finger with the sticky side out. Slip it off and pinch it flat.

Stick one side of the sticky tape to the back of the moustache. Press it onto your upper lip.

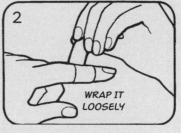

Stick some cotton balls onto a cardboard moustache or a piece of stiff material.

Beards

Beards can be a very useful disguise if they look real, because they cover up so much of your face.

Make this small goatee beard by sticking a cotton ball onto a triangle of fabric.

Thick sideburns made in the same way can make your face look quite different.

1 Bushy beard

Bend some wire or joined pipe cleaners to hook over your ears. Join a loop to go around your mouth.

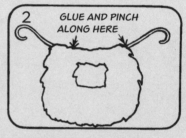

2 GLUE AND PINCH ALONG HERE

Lay a big piece of absorbant cotton over the frame. Fold it over and pinch it together with glue.

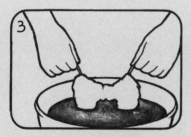

3

When the glue is dry, dip the beard in watery paint. Pull gently at the cotton to make it hairy.

4

Hang the beard up to dry by its wire ear hooks. Then it will be ready for use on your next mission.

Changing your hair

Another good way to change your appearance and make your disguise more real is to alter your hairstyle or make yourself a wig.

Brushing back

If your hair usually falls forward over your forehead, try brushing it back with water.

Brushing forward

If you usually brush your hair back or to one side, let it fall forward and hang over your eyes.

Change your parting

See what happens if you change your parting from one side to the other. You may look quite different.

In the middle

For a really funny look, part your hair down the middle. Even your friends may not recognize you.

Going white

A sprinkling of talcum powder will make your hair lighter. Wash or brush it out afterwards.

In the net

If you have long hair, push it up into a hairnet. This will disguise it altogether.

Wigs

1 Making a wig

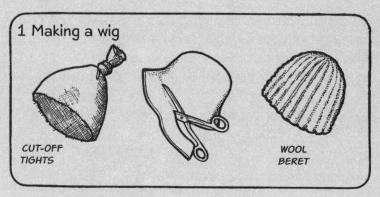

CUT-OFF TIGHTS

WOOL BERET

If you want to make a full wig, you must first find a base that fits your head and covers your own hair. This could be made from some cut-off tights, an old hat with the brim cut off, or a beret.

Stick or sew strands of wool or untwisted string onto the base. Remember to start at the bottom.

The top layers will overlap the bottom ones. Now trim the hair to the style you want.

The bald look

The easiest way to make yourself look bald is to wear a plain pink bathing cap which covers up all your own hair. For a nearly-bald look, stick strands of cotton around the sides of the cap.

Hats

Hats and scarves are useful disguises. Use them to hide part of your face or the shape of your head. Make a collection of different shapes and sizes. Always try to wear one that goes with the rest of your disguise.

All one hat

Think of different ways of wearing the same hat or cap. Push it to the back of your head. Turn it around to face the back or turn it inside out.

Bends

Shadows

Rain

Shine

Hats with wide brims are useful. Bend them into different shapes or hide your face in their shadow. Choose your hat for a secret mission carefully, and don't get caught out by a change in the weather.

False hair

1

Stick strands of cotton or string to the inside of a hat or scarf.

2

You can also use this method to hide your own hair.

Scarves

Turbans

If you have a long scarf, try making a turban. Wind it around and around. Then tuck the end in.

Scarves

Long scarves are also very useful for hiding most of your face from the Enemy.

1 Tying a headscarf

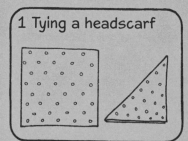

Here are three ways of tying a square headscarf. First fold it diagonally to make a triangle.

2

Lay the long edge over your head. Tie two ends under your chin. The third corner hangs at the back.

3

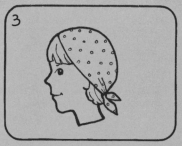

Lay the long edge over your head. Now take the two front ends and tie them at the back.

4

Put the long edge at the back and a point at your forehead. Tie the two ends on top of your head.

Change your voice

One of the easiest ways to recognize someone is by the sound of their voice. However well you disguise your face or body, your voice may give you away.

If you want to disguise your voice by using a particular accent, you will have to rehearse it a lot before you talk to people. Foreign accents are fun but you must keep it up without speaking in your normal voice. Try talking in very high and very low voices as well.

1 On the telephone

Hold a handkerchief over the mouthpiece. Call a friend who can tell you what you sound like.

2

Your voice will sound even more different if you purse your lips as if you are about to whistle.

3

If you hold your nose while you are speaking, your voice will sound very strange.

4

Now give a big smile. Curl your lips back to show your teeth. Your voice will change again.

The best ways of exposing a false voice are to make the suspect laugh or to give him a fright.

You could jump out from behind a tree. But make sure you don't give him too much of a shock.

If you need to pass a secret message, but you think you are being watched, don't look at the person you are talking to. Look at someone else or pretend to be doing something different.

Try whispering secret messages without moving your lips or looking at other people. Rehearse it in a public place such as a bus or train, until you can do it without anyone noticing.

Disguise scrapbook

You can have fun making a scrapbook of ideas for different disguises and good places to spy. This will help you to build up a collection of clothes and equipment ready for secret missions. Cut out pictures from comics, magazines and travel brochures and stick them into your book.

When you plan a secret mission, remember that neither your disguise nor what you do should attract attention. You must plan to fit in with your surroundings. The next few pages will give you some ideas for spying on other people and buildings without being noticed.

Working spies

A good time for spying, if you live in a town, is at rush hour in the morning or evening as people are going to work or returning home. There are always lots of people moving around carrying cases and reading papers.

No one has much time to notice anything else. If you are spying on a particular building, keep walking at the same pace as everyone else.

Summer spies

Even on a very hot day on the beach, when no one wears many clothes, it is possible to spy without being seen. Wear a sun hat and dark glasses. Choose a spot where you can see in all directions.

Winter spies

This is the easiest time for spying. Everybody is wrapped up in warm clothes. You can bend your head and shuffle along without being noticed. But keep moving, as no one stands still in the cold.

Bicycle spies

A bicycle is a very useful piece of equipment for moving around and spying without being noticed.

Pretend your bicycle has a puncture. It is a good excuse to get off and keep watch on a building.

More ideas for the scrapbook

1 Town spies

Some places in town, such as bus stops, are good for spying. People are often waiting so you are less likely to be noticed by the Enemy.

Another good place is a station. There are always lots of people around when trains arrive. If you sit quietly, you may not be noticed.

Sleeping spy

On a sunny day you can see people asleep in parks. Are they really asleep or spying?

Tourist spy

No one suspects tourists of spying. They can stroll around taking pictures and looking at everything.

1 Country spies

It is more difficult to spy in the country. You must have a good reason to be there or you'll look suspicious. Try some bird watching.

2

Some secret buildings are in the country. Disguise yourself as a hiker. You can pretend to rest and read a map without looking suspicious.

Spy pairs

Two people can often walk together without looking suspicious. A happy couple looks carefree and innocent.

Bad spies

Bad spies look obvious. Never pace up and down impatiently. People will wonder who you are.

Spy language

Camouflage Clothes worn by a spy which blend into the background so he or she is not noticed by the Quarry.

Code breaking Working out the clear meaning of a message in code without first knowing which code is used.

Contact A member of your spy ring, usually one you meet by arrangement.

Courier A member of a spy ring who carries and delivers secret messages, information or instructions to other members.

Cover Anything, such as buildings or bushes, which a spy uses to hide behind.

Decode To work out the clear meaning of a code message using a key or indicator.

Drop A place where messages are left by spies for other spies.

Encode Putting a message into a code.

False drop A place where you pretend to leave messages, or where you leave messages written in a Spoof Code.

Indicator An innocent-looking sign that shows where to find a message or how to decode it, or develop it.

Interception Getting hold of a message, or decoding a coded message, left by Enemy Spies.

Headquarters (H.Q.) The place, perhaps secret, a spy ring operates from.

Key A clue to the code used in a message, or the code itself.

Keyword A word with all different letters that is used to make a code.

Master Spy The head of a spy ring.

The Opposition The enemy spies.

Plain Message A message not written in code.

Quarry Someone who is secretly stalked, tracked or shadowed.

Rendezvous A meeting between two members of a spy ring.

Scrambled A code that works by mixing up the letters of a message in a special way is a scrambled code.

Shadowing Following and keeping watch on a Quarry in a town without him or her knowing.

Security Safety. When your messages and actions are well-disguised or well-hidden they are secure.

Signpost Part of a drop system where signs are left to show which drop is being used.

Spoof Code Letters jumbled up to look like a real code to fool Enemy Spies.

Spy Ring A group of spies who work together secretly.

Stalking Following a Quarry secretly by moving quietly through the countryside and staying hidden.

Substitution code A code that works by swapping message letters with the letters of a scrambled alphabet or a symbol alphabet.

Surveillance Keeping watch secretly on an Enemy Spy, or on a building which Enemy Spies use as their H.Q. or as a Rendezvous.

Suspect A person suspected of being a spy or a member of the Enemy.

Tail A spy who shadows another spy.

Tracking Following the tracks, clues or footprints left by a Quarry when he or she is out of sight.

Trail The tracks left accidentally by a Quarry, or the clues and messages left by a member or a spy ring for the Contact to follow.

Trainer An expert spy who teaches other spies useful skills.

Undercover Agent A spy operating in disguise in enemy territory.

Wash A mixture of water and ink or paint used to develop a wax or water message.

Answers

Answers to Who is the traitor?
Coded messages on pages
20 and 21
These messages show that Owl is
the new leader and Fox is the
traitor. Have you identified Owl
and Fox? Turn the page upside-
down to see the answer.

Paris calling Delhi (Rev-Group
Code) Our leader is caught. Owl is
second in command. Are you Owl?

Delhi calling Paris (Pendulum Code)
My code name is not Owl. The
traitor is Fox. Who is Fox?

Delhi calling Cairo (Bi-Rev Code)
Fox is a traitor. Bat knows him. I
am not Bat. Who is?

Cairo calling Delhi (Sandwich Code)
Code names should be secret, but
mine is neither Bat nor Fox.

Cairo calling Paris (Mid-null Code)
If you are Bat, do you know who
Fox is?

Paris calling Cairo (Rev-Group
Code) Elk may know who Fox is. I
am not Bat or Elk.

Cairo calling Helsinki (Rev-Random
Code) Fox has betrayed us. Talk to
Bat or Elk. I am neither.

Helsinki calling Cairo (Bi-Rev Code)
Owl will be our new leader. My code
name is not Owl.

Identity of traitor and new leader
on pages 20 and 21

The agent in Cairo has let it slip
that he is not Bat, Fox or Elk, so he
must be Owl, the new leader. The
agent in Paris cannot be Owl, and
he has said he is not Bat or Elk, so
he must be the traitor—Fox.

Answer to Code breaking practice on
page 26
The only 5-letter words between
one and seven are three and ten. Did
you guess that the first two words
of the message are 'The three'? If
so, you will have found that the
message is encoded with the 8-5
key of the code card. It reads:

The three new members of our spy
ring will meet us at headquarters
tonight.

Answers to Trail signs puzzle on pages 100 and 101

The place for learners is, of course, the school. Follow the arrows to the first message. The inn with the twinkly name is the North Star. Follow the arrows. At the Post Office crossroads, go in the opposite direction to the north.   To do this, look at the sign at the bottom right of the right-hand page and go south. Follow the arrows. Go to the other church. Follow the arrows. Go to the other pond — Druid's Pond. The sign there says 'your Contact has gone home'.

Answers to Indian messages on pages 104 and 105

1. Hide in the forest near the river.

2. No night meeting.

3. Bring rations to the campfire in the evening.

4. Meeting in the morning by the lake.

5. Enemy hidden near camp.

6. Leader of the enemy talks about peace.

7. People have discovered our hideout — flee.

Answers to Track puzzle on pages 110 and 111

The tracks coming from the right are those of a man walking his dog. The dog sees a cat at the top right and dashes off, dragging its lead. The cat climbs a tree and the dog waits below. Meanwhile, the man darts into the road after the dog, is hit by a motorcyclist. Motorcyclist rides off. Man at top left runs to help injured man to a chair brought by a lady from the house, middle top. Man coming from bottom left runs to telephone booth to call ambulance. Ambulance arrives. Injured man is helped into it by first helper, who climbs in too. Both drive off.

Answers to the Picking up a trail puzzle on pages 114 and 115

The Quarry has climbed over the gate and taken the path to the right of the clearing. There are five clues:

1. Footprint just in front of gate.

2. Mud scraped on bars of gate.

3. Birds flying up beyond the bushes on the right side of the clearing.

4. Cows staring along the right-hand path.

5. Birds and rabbits on the middle and left-hand paths feeding quietly.

Additional illustrations by:
John Jamieson, Liz Graham-Yooll
Juliet Stanwell-Smith

Cover design by Jamie Ball

This edition first published in 2014 by Usborne Publishing Ltd.,
Usborne House, 83-85 Saffron Hill, London EC1N 8RT, England.
www.usborne.com. Copyright © Usborne Publishing Ltd 2014,
2007, 1989, 1978. The name Usborne and the devices ♀ ⊕ are
Trade Marks of Usborne Publishing Ltd. All rights reserved.